The Caring Friend's Guide
to Bipolar Disorder

Martin Baker and Fran Houston

NORDLAND
www.nordlandpublishing.com

Copyright

High Tide, Low Tide © Baker & Houston 2016

Published by Nordland Publishing 2016

ISBN Print: 978-82-8331-021-4
ISBN E-book: 978-82-8331-022-1

Note: The authors write in their own distinct voices. In Fran's case this is American English. For Martin, it is British English. Spelling conventions have been preserved for both writers, with no attempt made to enforce consistency.

For the ill ones and the well ones

Friendship soothes the soul and provides hope for people with bipolar disorder and yet the illness creates unique challenges to the friendships we so desperately want and need. Marty and Fran specifically address these challenges in this bright, uplifting and brutally honest book. Filled with stories and practical tips, there is more laughter than sorrow as the reader learns to cultivate a loving, kind and caring friendship that transcends the illness and creates a lasting bond.

—Julie A. Fast, author of *Loving Someone with Bipolar Disorder*, *Take Charge of Bipolar Disorder*, and *Get it Done When You're Depressed*.

Contents

Foreword

As someone who has suffered from debilitating depression, and now writes about mental health, there is one question I am nearly always asked by those who come to my talks and workshops. What is my advice for those who are caring for someone with a mental illness? What is the best way to be a true and supportive friend? I've often thought if only there was a book I could recommend. Martin Baker and Fran Houston have now written just such a book.

Written in Martin's compassionate, conversational and intimate style, with a powerful introductory piece by Fran in which she sets the scene and explains her life as someone who suffers from chronic fatigue syndrome, fibromyalgia and bipolar disorder, the authors recount their journey as friends since they first met online in May 2011. At the time Fran was living on an island in Maine, USA, and Martin was based in Newcastle upon Tyne in the North of England.

Martin found himself on the social media page of someone who was suicidal. Hundreds of people had posted well-meaning comments and he added one of his own: "Flooding light and love into your world." Someone called Fran Houston responded almost immediately. "Sometimes even too much love can be overwhelming."

As Martin recalls, "The comment intrigued and unsettled me." He realized that some of the responses were less about the person who was so unwell and more about the respondents' own need for reassurance. A thought-provoking correspondence with Fran ensued. As Fran put it, many of the comments were "nothing about her and what she needs.. all about what others want to give her." A thoughtful, loving, humorous and at times painful friendship was born and this wonderful book is the result.

The book recounts in Martin's words what it is to befriend someone who is ill, initially online, and then face-to-face. It shares his wisdom and gentleness and what he's learnt about helping a friend, as well as what he's learnt from Fran. The invitation is always to be adventurous, to explore and to be different. In the authors' words, "Be who you are, do what you can, and embrace the journey." I particularly agreed with the advice that "Baby steps are steps too." This is a particular belief of mine and the reason I wrote about my own 52 small steps to happiness in one of my books.

This book is a brilliant practical guide to understanding your friend's diagnosis and symptoms, the reality of treatments and therapies, and how to overcome the challenges of long-distance communication. More than that, it is a book about what friendship means. I loved the description of Martin's netbook perched on top of his saucepan stand as he cooked Christmas dinner and comforted Fran at the same time. But there's nothing sentimental or clichéd about this book: the authors confront the dangers of becoming codependent and what to do when your friend is suicidal.

Such are the questions I am often asked in my role as a mental health campaigner and as an ambassador for Sane, Rethink, and Young Minds, as well as in a more personal capacity. I'm very happy that this book now provides so many answers. I congratulate the authors on finding the courage to write it. In doing so, they will have helped themselves, but more importantly, will help many others too.

Rachel Kelly
The Lake District, England
July 2016

Rachel Kelly, author of *Black Rainbow: How words healed me: my journey through depression* and *Walking on Sunshine: 52 Small Steps to Happiness*, is a journalist, mental health campaigner, and Ambassador for SANE and Rethink Mental Illness.

Preface

Writing has always been an important part of my life. I remember the teacher who encouraged me by providing a notebook for my extracurricular stories. I remember being snubbed by my classmates for asking if I could submit a poem in place of the expected essay: our teacher thought it such a good idea he set poetry for the entire class. I remember volunteering as assistant editor on the school magazine because I had a crush on the teacher. I remember the yellowing copy of Ezra Pound's poetry I borrowed from the library and neglected to return. I wrote poetry through sixth form (my final two years at school) and university; later essays, articles, and short stories. I have kept a personal diary for over forty years.

A keen science student, I studied pharmacy at the University of Bradford, Yorkshire. I graduated in 1983 and took up a postgraduate position at the Department of Neurology, Institute of Psychiatry and King's College Hospital Medical School in London. In 1987, I moved north to work in the biomedical sciences laboratory at Newcastle's Royal Victoria Infirmary. I met my wife Pam that same year. I later retrained in business computing and have worked in the information technology services industry ever since.

I met Fran Houston online in May 2011. Fran lives with bipolar disorder, chronic fatigue syndrome, and fibromyalgia, and we joke that when she discovered I was a pharmacy graduate with three years' research experience in neuroscience she thought all her worries were over. Here at last was someone to sort her life out for her! In fact, little I had learned in the lecture theatre or laboratory prepared me to help someone living with chronic, debilitating illness. Education is extremely valuable—I have completed a number of courses and workshops since meeting Fran which help me support her more effectively—but ultimately caring is not about how much you know, it is about who you are and what you do.

This book was conceived in October 2012. During a phone call with Fran I mentioned that I felt inspired to do something creative. Without hesitation, she suggested I write a book about befriending someone who lives with illness. The idea made a great deal of sense. Despite living three thousand miles apart, we had forged a relationship that was strong, caring, and mutually rewarding. I saw immediately that my experience could be of value to others. But if the suggestion was inspired, it was also scary. My first thought was that I had never looked on her as "someone living with illness." I saw her as my friend.

> That is the point, Marty! It is how you are with me. People do not usually treat me that way once they know I have illness. It is a powerful thing. It has helped me see that I am not just my illnesses. I have value and gifts to give.

In the weeks that followed, we discussed possible approaches, formats, and the likely audience for such a book. I researched similar titles, made notes, and sketched outlines. The further I pursued the idea the more it eluded me. I could see the book only as an autobiographical account of our friendship, and while that could be a tale worth telling, it wasn't what Fran had envisaged. I began to lose heart. Our conversations turned to other topics and the idea of the book lapsed.

One night in late November, Fran telephoned me. It was four o'clock in the morning here in the UK. She was very excited. She had been to dinner with someone who wanted advice on how to support a friend diagnosed with bipolar disorder. Fran offered suggestions from her own experience, and mentioned she knew someone in England who was writing a book on that very subject. Her friend thought it was a great idea and wanted to know when the book would be published. My heart sank. Too sleepy to be anything but honest, I told Fran what I had come to realise, but had not until that moment shared with her. Our book was never going to happen. Fran didn't press me for details or explanations. She said goodnight and let me get back to sleep.

I went to work next day as usual, and avoided thinking about our conversation until I was walking to catch the train home. It was a shame nothing would come of Fran's idea. My thoughts turned to a book on depression I had recently finished reading. Written by a clinical psychologist, it had an easy style and was illustrated with snippets of conversation. It was nothing like the book Fran and I had talked about, but could a similar approach work for us? Something clicked. I messaged Fran from the train.

Thank you for mentioning our book to your friend last night, for telling me about her reaction to the idea, and for the response it stirred in me. It was the jolt I needed. Just now, in the very act of repeating to myself how our book will never come into being, I caught a glimpse of how it might. I want to rededicate myself to the project. I want to start making notes, drafting ideas. I want to write.

It was a breakthrough moment, and one utterly in keeping with the central message of the book you are holding. No matter what happens or what you are struggling with—be that some practical or creative project, your relationship with others, your own health or that of a loved one—the important thing is to set aside preconceived notions of how things should be, or whether you are up to the task. Instead, be honest with yourself about what is happening. Acknowledge your limitations, but refuse to be bound by them. Trust in your ability to grow to meet the challenge. Recognise joyfully the potential of each moment.

Be who you are. Do what you can. Embrace the journey.

Martin Baker
Newcastle upon Tyne, UK

Acknowledgements

We are grateful to writer, journalist, and mental health campaigner Rachel Kelly for her encouragement and support, and for contributing the foreword to our book. We thank those who permitted us to quote from personal messages and correspondence: Anne Pringle, Ansi James, Bernadette Barnes, Bridget Woodhead, Bob Keyes, Charlotte Walker, Dara Hurt, Franni C. Vitolo, Howard Baldwin, Lin Downing, Lisa Overall, and Maya Hayward. Likewise, those who offered advance endorsements, including Cheryl Ramsay, Megan Cyrulewski, and Stefanie Cary. Your belief that we had something valuable to share kept us going through the periods of self-doubt, setbacks, and uncertainty that will be familiar to any writer.

Special thanks are due to those who gave their time to read or edit our manuscript, including Creighton Taylor, Donna Betts, Donna Murphy, Jackie Charley, Julie A. Fast, Rachel Thompson, and Wendy K. Williamson. Your honesty, suggestions, and advice helped us refine our ideas and approach throughout the creative process. This book is the richer for your contributions.

We are eternally grateful to Michael Kobernus, Markus Furchner, and the team at Nordland Publishing, for taking a chance on us and welcoming us into the Nordland family.

We acknowledge and thank Fran's professional care team, including Aaron Cloutier, Avner Eisenberg, Dr. Christina Holt, Cicely Matz, Dr. George McNeil, Heather Small, John Turrell, Julie Goell, Michael Gelsanliter, and Dr. William Jeanblanc.

We thank our families for putting up with us over the four years it has taken to bring this project to fruition, especially Martin's wife Pam for her unwavering love and support, and their children Emma and Mike. It is to Mike we owe our introduction to Nordland Publishing. Fran thanks her mother Christa and sister Veronica for being there always. Words are inadequate to express our gratitude and love for our friends, so we simply say thank you to you all, especially Abby, Andrea, Barry, BB, Bob, Chris, Howard, Jim, James, Jeanne, Jomo, Lara, Laurel, Lin, Maya, and Peg.

We are grateful for those who inspire us and enrich our lives simply by being who they are, including Andy Behrman, Angela Slater, Brené Brown, Carrie Fisher, Claire Stewart, Darren Hodge, Deepak Chopra, Diane Atwood, Eckhart Tolle, Gabe Howard, Gayathri Ramprasad, Geneen Roth, Jessie Close, John Cariani, Jon Kabat-Zinn, Kay Redfield Jamison, Kristy Schell, Laura Hillenbrand, Oprah Winfrey, Patty Duke, Sarah Fader, Sherry Joiner, Snatam Kaur, and Steven Heslewood.

We acknowledge the many groups and organisations we have encountered, all dedicated to countering stigma and supporting those affected by mental and invisible illness, including Bring Change 2 Mind, Bipolar UK, Family Hope, Men Tell Health, MIND, NAMI Maine, The NoStigmas Network, Rethink Mental Illness, SANE, Stigma Fighters, and Time to Change.

Finally, we would like to thank the thousands of you who follow us on our blog, website, and social media platforms. Whether you are moved to comment and share our content, or quietly accompany us on our journey, you have meant—and mean—the world to us. This book is for you.

Introduction

We are all ill and well
We are all friend and family
—Fran Houston

Not All Sunshine and Rainbows

Life isn't all sunshine and rainbows, Fran. If it's real, if it has
any depth or meaning at all, there are going to be edges and
raw places. It's not my job to protect you from them, just as
it's not your job to protect me. It's our job, as friends, to be
together in the darkness and the dirt, so we know we are
not alone.

This book describes what it is like to be in a caring relationship
with someone who lives with mental illness. Specifically, what it is
like for me—Martin—and my best friend Fran who lives on the
other side of the world and is diagnosed with bipolar disorder,
chronic fatigue syndrome, and fibromyalgia. Despite Fran's
courage and humour, and my natural—some might say
pathological—optimism, there is much that challenges us. Mania,
depression, debilitating pain, fatigue, and suicidal thinking all have
their place in Fran's life and in our relationship. We face them
together. This book explores how we do so, and how *you* can be
there for your friend.

Maybe it is not a friend but your partner, sibling, parent, or
child. Whatever the nature of your relationship it is likely to be
long-term and committed. If you are reading this book, you are
looking for something. Perhaps you have specific questions you
want answered. Maybe you need practical solutions and
suggestions, or simply hope to find something relevant to what
you are going through. Or perhaps you are the one living with
illness and want to understand how things are for those who care
about you. Maybe you have a general interest in illness and well-
being, personal development and growth, or the dynamics of

long-distance relationships. Whoever you are, we believe our book will help you. The lessons we have learned, the experiences we have shared, are here for you. *We* are here for you.

Why This Book Is Different

Many books describe the impact of mental illness on those who are ill and the people who care for them. (You will find a selection of titles we find especially moving, insightful, and helpful in the appendix.) None, however, perfectly match the needs of friends who want to make a difference but are unsure what to do. Autobiographies shed light on what it means to live with illness but offer little in the way of practical guidance. Workbooks educate about symptoms and treatments, but they tend to be generic in approach and are aimed at the person who is ill. "Friends and families" books focus almost exclusively on partners and close family members. Crucially, given that friends and family often live far apart, no current titles describe how to support someone who lives at a distance, whether in another town, state, or country. We hope our book will inform and inspire you. There are no steps you have to follow, or things that are guaranteed to work under all circumstances. Illness, especially mental illness, does not work that way. What works is having a framework of trust and commitment, and a menu of approaches, suggestions, and options you and your friend can explore together. Connection is vital, whether you live on the same street or on opposite sides of the world. No one is too far away to be cared for, or to care.

Key Messages

We wrote this book with three key messages in mind. First, you do not need special skills or experience to support your friend. Second, you can make a huge difference to your friend's life and help to counter the stigma that still surrounds mental health issues. Third, there is a great deal to celebrate!

Be Yourself

I knew very little about mental illness before I met Fran. I have learned a great deal since then, and I am still learning. It is okay to be less than perfect, because none of us are. It is okay to get things wrong sometimes; we all do that. It is okay to become upset and frustrated; we all feel like that from time to time. What counts is showing up, having the courage to be honest with yourself and with your friend about what is happening, and finding a way through to the other side.

Be There

Organisations, including The National Institute of Mental Health in the US and the Mental Health Foundation (the UK's leading mental health charity) estimate that one in five adults have a mental health problem in any given year, with a quarter of those experiencing a serious mental illness. Extending that to friends and family, it is hard to find anyone unaffected in some way.

I talk openly about my experiences as Fran's friend. Almost without exception, the people I talk to respond positively. Most are intrigued and supportive. Many offer stories in return, telling me of their own mental health concerns, or those of friends, partners, or family members. There are signs mental illness is no longer the taboo it once was, but there is still a long way to go and no room for complacency. Many people continue to suffer stigma and social isolation if they admit to—or are unable to hide—mental health issues. My wife describes what happened when she spoke at work about her previous breakdown.

> They looked at me in disgust. Five minutes earlier I had been good enough. Now I had fallen from grace. Sometime afterwards I wanted to find new employment. I wrote three times for references but none of my letters were answered. I was disgusted, upset and angry that they could be so judgmental when I had been honest with them. I am not ashamed of my breakdown now, but I was made to feel that way at the time.

One of the most devastating misconceptions is that mental illness renders people incapable of maintaining meaningful relationships. While researching this book we read of a man whose girlfriend had been diagnosed with bipolar disorder. She broke up with him because her therapist told her she could never have a deep relationship with anyone. She was twenty-eight years old. Fran has faced her share of stigma and rejection.

> I still need reminding I can have lasting relationships, with some of the rejection I have had.. I thank everyone who doesn't leave when I am suffering particularly severe symptoms.. Many do leave and it hurts.. Every time.. But there are those who stay no matter what.. They are gold..

We cannot set the world right, but by sharing our experiences we add our voices to those challenging stigma and discrimination. Your relationship with your friend can likewise be a beacon of light. Simply by being there and not turning away, by responding with kindness and empathy instead of negativity and rejection, you help your friend feel worthy and less alone. As Fran puts it, "Friendship is good medicine and being present is the greatest gift of all."

Celebrate the Positive

It might seem naive to talk of celebrating the positive. The pain, heartache, despair, and danger associated with mental illness are very real. Sometimes all you can do is to hang in there together. But that is not all there is. The idea that it will be a nightmare for the healthy one in the relationship needs challenging, because that is not how it is for me. In our time as friends, we have confronted many of our personal doubts and fears. We have learned that illness and distance are not the barriers to successful relationships they might appear to be. The journey is hard at times, but it is also fun, rich, and deeply fulfilling. I have gained a deeper awareness of who I am as a person, and discovered I can make a difference to the lives of others. That is worth celebrating.

How This Book Is Organised

Written in simple, non-technical language, we have organised this book into three parts around our guiding message: "Be who you are. Do what you can. Embrace the journey." Each chapter opens with a question and answer section. Parts I and II explore how to build and maintain a successful caring relationship, the nature of illness and wellness, and how to be there for your friend through good times and bad. In part III, we share the most challenging period in our relationship to date, and demonstrate how we use these ideas and approaches on a day-to-day basis. And finally, the appendix provides resources for further reading and support.

Perspective and Language

This book is presented from my (Martin's) point of view as the supportive friend. In Fran's words, "The perspective needs to be yours rather than mine, because there are many stories from ill ones and so few from friends who care." Her voice, opinions, and personality are clearly expressed in the many quotations and conversations included, as well as the poems introducing each part of the book. Furthermore, Fran's autobiographical essay, "Lessons of the Night," sheds light on her life before we met.

Sources and Editing

We have drawn extensively on our archive of e-mail and text messages, instant message (chat) conversations, and other documents including my personal diary. Our aim has been to preserve the authentic nature of our conversations—including our respective UK and US spellings and language—but we have corrected gross spelling and grammatical mistakes, and expanded chat acronyms and abbreviations. Fran considers her idiosyncratic use of language and punctuation (most notably her use of the double period ".." and lower case personal pronoun "i") to be aspects of her illness and personality. In most cases these are presented unchanged. Friends and members of Fran's professional support team are generally not named. However, all persons mentioned are real. Some names have been changed.

The Language of Illness

Words reflect how we think and feel about ourselves and the world, and how we are perceived by others. This is especially true when talking about illness, wellness, and recovery. We wrote this book using language that works for us. We hope you will be inspired to consider how you and your friend talk about illness, and its impact on each of you.

The Ill Ones and the Well Ones

Well or ill, we are all people. Nevertheless, it is naive, disrespectful, and dangerous to downplay the impact illness has on those affected by it. Those who are ill are often treated differently—and poorly—compared to those that society considers able-bodied and (especially) able-minded. In consequence, they have particular life experiences, perceptions, expectations, and needs. To use Fran's terminology, she is the ill one in our relationship; I am the well one. Nothing more or less is implied by our use of these terms.

My Bipolar Best Friend

Of Fran's diagnosed conditions, bipolar disorder has the greatest impact on our friendship. We describe the different bipolar types in chapter 2, but use the generic term throughout the book. Fran's preferred term for someone who lives with bipolar disorder is bipolarist, although this is not in common use. We dislike phrases such as "Fran suffers from bipolar disorder," preferring to say she lives with—or has, or is diagnosed with—bipolar disorder. I sometimes refer to her as "my bipolar friend," but never as "a bipolar." It is interesting to note that illness affects how Fran describes her own situation.

> When I am ill I usually say "I am manic" or "I am depressed." Or sometimes "I have depression." When I am not ill I refer to having been "in mania" or "in depression."

Summary

Ultimately, this book is not about me and Fran at all. It is not about bipolar disorder, or even about illness. It is about being friends and accepting your friend for who they are, rather than as someone defined by their illness, situation, or other issues. It is about embracing the journey you take together, one step at a time.

Lessons of the Night

Sometimes I wake up. Sometimes not. I hold onto the bed for dear life. I am familiar with the night and its darkness. As a child I lived in the basement of our house as a mole does in his tunnel and could navigate through the narrow path of jagged, stacked boxes to the bathroom in the dark. The lights didn't work.

Wrapped in my blanket of night, I am safe and warm. In the night are dreams. Dreams of all the things that can't be done in my body because of its restrictions of fatigue and pain. I indulge my soul's longing to fly.

The day hurts my eyes with its stinging brightness. Music hurts my ears with its loudness and overstimulation. I like the quiet of night.

I have chronic fatigue syndrome, fibromyalgia, and bipolar disorder. They operate as independent sine waves. At any time, I can be exhausted and manic, energized and depressed. Every combination imaginable. The cycles can last for days or months or even years. It's an odd assortment.

I had a mate. I had a family. I had a home. I had a career. I had a dog. I lost them all.

I made $14,000 in the last week I worked in the real world as an electrical engineer. Now I barely make that in a year. Fifteen years ago, I paid tens of thousands of dollars to get my health back, conventionally and alternatively. It took ten years to get an accurate diagnosis. Treating bipolar with antidepressants makes it much worse. So not fun to have cfs and fibro creep in alongside.

I finally went to the backwoods of Maine for a year and lived in a camp on 189 acres with no running water and no electricity—an attempt to find my baseline, fight my demons and find the night, or die. No TV, no radio, no books, no writing, no nothing. Just me and myself, grapes and garlic. I danced naked in the woods in the pouring rain. I shoveled snow thirty feet out to the outhouse to go to the bathroom. I made snow angels under the full moon. I watched frost form on the windows. I gazed for hours at the cherry wallpaper. I slept twenty hours a day. I dropped each thought as though dropping a hot coal. I'd think the same thought again; drop the thought again, over and over. I would not get up until I felt the internal impulse to do so. I fasted. I had a sauna each week—the only excursion besides getting water from a spring. And successfully navigated men who were intrigued and unsavory. I reached the edge of madness. I waited for the Jesus experience. There is no god; there is just life that flows. There is no hope. That was the beginning. Stop the search. For god. For healing. Just stop. The maple tree doesn't want to be an oak. They are what they are.

I moved to an island off the coast of Maine in September 2003. My dad died that Halloween night—the night when the veil between the world of the real and the unreal is thinnest. There was an aurora borealis that evening. Beauty without effort.

I lost my mind. Consumed with thoughts of jumping off the boat, a frustrated friend asked, "Why don't you?" I panicked.

I found the psychiatrist I still see now. He doesn't see anyone anymore, but the deal was that I agreed to be in a fishbowl where he trained six to eight other psychiatrists for twelve sessions, and then I would have him for life. He is very conservative with meds, which I am very grateful for, although at times it's enraged me. I think that psychiatrists nowadays are too pill pushy. Meds take a long time before you can see any results. One has to courageously wade through a myriad of side effects. He also is very relationship-oriented, which few are. He is respectful of me as a human being not just as a patient. Also, making an eye-to-eye commitment to him to stay alive has been a critical component of the process.

I began intensive group therapies. I got pissed off a lot. It was a full time job. I was exhausted. I was depressed. Having to do all this work. Needing to do all this work. No hope of getting better. Homework. It was worse than Engineering school. Cognitive Behavior Therapy made sense though. Event. Feelings. Thoughts behind feelings. Change the thoughts. Huh. Seeing others who'd been stuck in their ruts changing. Me changing. Huh. Not so depressed. My mind actually thinking thoughts other than depressed ones. How refreshing.

Chronic fatigue syndrome can mean days or months bedridden. Or can be as simple as feeling like there are cotton balls behind my eyes and mud running in my veins. Pain is always present. I take Advil when it is too much, or something else. I see an osteopath, acupuncturist, and chiropractor regularly. Once when I was at dinner with a friend I fell asleep. They ushered me out of there swiftly. I've been propped up in lazy boys in the corner with a blanket at parties just to be able to attend. Then again friends have broken up with me because of my proclivity to say no, or act strange. As a fellow cfs-er puts it, "I feel minimally crappy today."

Bipolar I is like mowing the lawn in the winter naked. I have bipolar II. An example of my mania is when I was out in front of my home on the phone talking wicked fast with a depressive friend, and I was frantically picking the heads off dandelions while every square inch of countertop in my home was littered with furiously ink-covered yellow stickies full of ideas and things to do and be and dreams. I am like a pit bull with a bone. Another example is when I found out about the United Nations International Day of Persons with Disabilities on December 3. I found out that VSA (Very Special Arts) out of Washington had a video that would be shown in seventeen countries internationally. My mania launched me into a full-blown attempt to notify media and government outlets seeking coverage for this event. I sent cryptic, confusing e-mails and was very agitated. I wasn't very successful, and thought that those who I contacted thought I was a nutcase. I felt like a mouse when a cat is playing with it and then the mouse just lies there stunned.

Depression was my best friend, the one I was most comfortable with. It's been a lifelong companion. A favorite blankie. The one I return to for wisdom. Deep and dark. I remember the pain of trying to wash a fork amongst all the dirty dishes in my sink, wrapping myself in a blanket, wearing clothes that hadn't been washed in a month, then opening a can of tuna and sitting on the cold floor to eat it. I told a depressed, suicidal friend once that it took more courage to make a cup of tea than to kill yourself. I still do have a stash of pills because I do feel that people should have that right, especially when you are old and everyone else is making decisions for you.

The problem/blessing with my illnesses is that they are unseen by the naked eye. "But you look fine," is the response, as if arguing with me would help. I was going to write my behind-the-scenes story in the *Island Times*. I talked with a friend about it—a friend who I had "iguana-sat" for during a time of deep depression, where basically the "iguana" saved my life because I had to feed it every day and felt responsible for it, and was therefore not free to commit suicide. The friend was scared of being exposed on the island and advised me to not tell my story publicly. I didn't. That is the kind of stigma that exists with disability.

I got to go to Hawaii because of a cat. They have quarantine rules and a friend moved there, and was delayed in bringing her cat and asked if I could escort him and stay for six weeks. I didn't blink twice before saying yes. It was beyond my wildest expectations. Some friends gave me mad money and the deal was that I couldn't do anything responsible with it, so when I was in Kauai I went for a helicopter ride, in the front seat, right next to the pilot, and you could look straight down. I wanted him to teach me to fly. I was so jazzed. Oh, the cliffs, the valleys, the ocean, the waterfalls, the rainbows. It was magnificent. It was absolutely the most amazing experience in my life. Even better than in my dreams.

The librarian on the island asked me to sit with an elder. So I started sitting with older islanders, and it was wonderful. They told me stories. I lived on the front of the island by the ferry boat slip, a great view. I bought a camera and took pictures of the sunsets.

I was frustrated. I wanted to somehow capture the elders' stories and share them. I went to an exhibit of black and white photographs and storyboards. My heart lit up with a flame so intense. I had never experienced that before. I knew what to do. I spoke with our little art gallery on the island about doing an exhibit. I spoke with the *Island Times* about doing a column to advertise for the exhibit. At the June exhibit everyone asked, "Where's the book?" So that began another journey. Mind you, I could only work a maximum of three hours a day. And I would have bouts of depression throughout. And bouts of freaked-out-ed-ness. I leaned on my friends and the community to help me. I busily interviewed and photographed islanders for another two years. Another gallery on the mainland offered to host the book launch/exhibit. In June of 2010 the book launched. By August it sold out. It's now in its second printing. I never started out thinking I would write a book. If someone had told me that, I never would've started. I would have been too scared. Even as I write this today on Christmas Eve 2010, I have friends who are coming to help me clean my little 18 x 18 home next week because I cannot manage it on my own.

This project was such a community effort. This island has given me so much. When I first got here I was amazed at its kindness towards me. I was broken and it loved me. So I wanted to give back by doing this project. I was surprised to find that again I was the receiver. As I sat and listened to the stories of my "lovies" as I called them, they taught me. Some of them have limited lives, pain, memory loss, reliance on others for care. I learned how to live my life fuller. I learned grace, courage, and how to have a twinkle in my eye. My chronic fatigue syndrome and depression limit me, but I can choose to live as fully as I want within those windows and be thankful. One thing we all do is get old. We can be wise to learn how to live our lives now.

"What's your next project?" I hated that question more than anything. I hadn't been able to do anything for ten years and could hardly stand up, let alone conceive of doing anything else for the rest of my life. Nobody really knew what toll this had taken on me, but I present well. My pat answer became, "I'm going to take a lot of naps," which I did until I went into a major depression for the beautiful month of August. I don't have seasonal affective disorder. I can be perfectly miserable in gorgeous weather and happy as a clam in the bitter cold or damp fog or pouring rain. That's clinical depression.

"How are you?" Another hated and seemingly innocuous question. The simple answer is F–I–N–E. F**ked up, insecure, neurotic, emotional. Most friends really don't want the long answer. This way I can simply smile and be honest gracefully.

I still have chronic fatigue syndrome. I still have fibromyalgia. I still have bipolar. I manage them. They don't manage me. They are a part of the package instead of who I am. I've learned to live alongside them, as esteemed companions, my teachers. Step by step, thought by thought, moment by moment. A little flame, follow it. Lessons of the night. I have this very simple view of life now. The good and bad come and go. Don't hold onto anything. I love the moment. Every bit of it. That's all I have. Heart wide open. It doesn't matter if someone kicks you; just point yourself in the direction you want to go. As far as god, I don't know. How can there not be?

The edges of the night are the best. Sunset, when the light slips below the horizon. That one moment taking the light over the rim of the earth, and rest comes. After which, the colors swell and dreams begin.

Fran Houston
Peaks Island, Maine
December 2010

Postscript

This was the first piece I ever wrote, and chronicles some of my journey of illness and how my creative endeavor helped me emerge from the hole, to know and experience a bigger life of possibility and change. Months after it was written I experienced my most delirious mania, followed by the most hellacious depression ever. Thankfully I had a hand to hold.

Part I: Be Who You Are

A Wild Hair

We are all creators and creation and creative
We are all students and teachers
We are all rich and poor
We are all leaders and followers
We are all homeless and homefull
We are all ill and well
We are all friend and family
We all have the power to give and love
We all came in naked
Babies
We all leave naked
We came with nothing
We leave with nothing
We are no better and no worse than each other
Never ever judge no one
Be and give
Then do from that place
Enemies are friends always in all ways
They teach too
There are no comparisons
No favorites
Only lessons
Learn well
Deep well
Simply love every thing
Be kind
Be open
Be wild free real
The long and short
Of it
Spir it
In my humble opinion
I'm just frannie
With a wild hair

1. The Caring Friendship: Key Skills and Attitudes

The measure of us is that I have grown to trust myself with you, and to trust yourself with me.
—Martin Baker

"What Is the Secret of Your Friendship?"

Fran has bipolar disorder, chronic fatigue syndrome, and fibromyalgia. We live three thousand miles apart, and at the time of writing have only met once face-to-face. We nevertheless have a close, mutually supportive friendship. How have we done this? Is there a secret? No. There really is nothing special about us! We are friends, and like friends the world over we handle what comes up as best we can. But while there is no great secret to share, there are qualities which are crucial to our success as friends. We trust each other, we are open and honest, and we love to connect.

We Trust Each Other

Fran trusts me to check her e-mail if she is unable to access it herself, to administer her websites and social media pages, and to monitor her mobile phone and Internet usage when she is travelling. We have each shared much of our personal history and experiences. Most fundamentally, Fran trusts me to be there for her, to be on her side, to fight her corner, and to always have her best interests at heart. For my part, I trust that I will handle whatever might come up. That doesn't mean I can deal with any situation or crisis on my own. We each recognise there are limits to our abilities and responsibilities. I carry a copy of Fran's wellness plan (see chapter 3) with me at all times. This includes contact details for her support team—close friends, doctor, psychiatrist, and care coordinator—should I ever find myself out of my depth.

We Are Open and Honest

We believe it is healthier to be open about our thoughts and feelings than to dismiss, hide, or avoid them. We share what is happening with us, discuss things if we need to, and then move on. In doing so, we hold a safe space where we can "let it all out." We sometimes get upset or angry with each other, but we deal with discord promptly if it occurs, recognising there is no need to fear even powerful emotions when they can be explored safely. It is fair to say such forthright honesty has caused problems for Fran with other people at times, especially during periods of mania when she is less respectful of social niceties. Not everyone appreciates having someone else's openness thrust in their face.

We Love to Connect

It is fundamental to the success of our friendship that we enjoy each other's company. We love to communicate and use all means available to us. Telephone and video calls, e-mails, text messages, letters, instant messaging, and other social media—each medium has its virtues, and adds its particular spice to our conversations. "Talking about stuff" will not cure your friend or solve all your relationship problems, but it will give you a greater chance of weathering the storms together. We take a closer look at how we keep in touch in chapter 4.

Perhaps the greatest obstacle to communicating effectively is the belief it should be easy. When you think about it, it is amazing anyone manages to communicate anything meaningful at all. Each of us has our unique mix of thoughts and feelings, hopes, fears, joys, pains, plans, worries, and views about how the world works. We scarcely understand them ourselves, yet we hope to share them with someone who has their own mix to contend with. And the only tools we have are the sounds we can utter, and the marks we can make on paper or a computer screen. It is no wonder we struggle at times! Approach your friend on the basis that you are each doing the best you can. Be gentle with yourself and with each other when things are not flowing well, and celebrate when they are. Good or bad, keep the channels open.

Six Mantras

We have built up a collection of sayings, or mantras, that we return to again and again as verbal shorthand for the principles they embody.

- Don't worry about me. Care for me.
- No pedestals.
- Baby steps are steps too.
- Feel it. Claim it. Love it. Let it go.
- Care but don't crowd. Share but don't pollute.
- Open hands. Open arms. Open heart.

Don't Worry about Me. Care for Me.

This is one of the first things I remember Fran telling me, and it is as relevant today as it was then. The phrases "I worry about you" and "I care for you" are often used interchangeably, but there are three important differences. When we care for a friend we are expressing our trust in their abilities, strengths, and resilience. We trust ourselves to support them as best we can, and trust others to contribute as they are able. We do not feel we have to do it all on our own, fix everything, or find all the answers. When we worry about a friend we express fear that they lack the resources to meet whatever challenges they are facing. We fear we don't know what we are doing, that we will be found lacking, or not up to the task. We fear others will not be around to contribute, and we will be left doing everything ourselves.

When we care we are focused on our friend's needs and how best we can help them meet those needs. Worry is focused primarily on our own needs: our need to be perceived as loving and giving, or our need for the problem to go away as quickly as possible so we can get back to normal. Worry tends to focus on the past (what has happened before in similar circumstances to us, to our friend, or to others) or the future (what might happen). Care focuses on what our friend needs in the present moment.

In the early days of our friendship Fran was manic, wild, and unpredictable. Many people—including some who had known her a long time—were fearful and worried about her behaviour. I was unsure whether my ability to remain calm in her presence was healthy, or a sign that I was ill-equipped to support her effectively. The following is from my diary.

> I never know how Fran is doing, not really. She can seem so fragile, so close to the edge, so hurt and hurting . . . and then the next moment we are laughing, or mad at each other. I'm learning not to be scared, not to worry, but instead to care. So many people are scared for her. They can't deal with her, can't cope at all. Perhaps I should be like that. Am I a danger to Fran because I am so calm? Perhaps I am being naive. Or perhaps it makes me precisely who she needs.

That final sentence was the turning point in my understanding. Positive, supportive and vigilant care is far healthier for Fran than any amount of fear-based worrying.

No Pedestals

No relationship can flourish if there is a perceived difference in stature or status. It is important to remember that we are all human, all fallible, all flawed. As Fran puts it so well, "We are all perfectly imperfect." Despite recognising the dangers, we have each been guilty on occasion of putting the other on a pedestal. I am a great support to Fran, and offer a degree of commitment she has rarely known. It was easy in the early days of our friendship for her to see me as some sort of hero or saviour figure.

> Fran: you are my world.. you are.. my life.. the reason.. of it.. all.. how how how.. do i deserve you..?
>
> Martin: Don't make me into more than I am, Frannie.
>
> Fran: ok ok.. for you no pedestal.. you are an oak.. rooted.. grounded..

Fran's spirit, courage, and resilience have occasionally led me to put her on a pedestal of her own, a situation complicated by her inclination to compare herself unfavourably to other people in terms of health, relationship status, financial security, and social standing. I counter her sense of unworthiness and inferiority, but I have sometimes overcompensated, boosting her mood and self-image unrealistically. At such times, "No pedestals!" reminds us we are in unhealthy territory. It is worth highlighting that there is a difference between putting people on pedestals and the distinction of client–therapist or patient–clinician roles in professional relationships. But I am neither Fran's therapist nor her doctor. I am her friend. We work best when we stand side by side, feet planted firmly on the same ground.

Baby Steps Are Steps Too

This is one of our favourites. It reminds us to stay focused in the present moment, to take life one step at a time, and to acknowledge that even the smallest advance counts as progress. Fran is very goal-oriented, and becomes frustrated if she seems to be straying off course or failing to make fast enough progress. In depression, this can reach a point where she despairs of ever achieving her targets or even progressing further towards them. At such times, "Baby steps are steps too" reminds her that she rarely stays stuck for long. She will try new ideas, or re-visit old ones, until something happens to move her forward.

Feel It. Claim It. Love It. Let It Go.

It can be challenging to handle powerful emotions, especially when they seem to come out of nowhere. Rather than allowing our emotions free rein, or trying to deny them, we find it helps to accept what we feel, take whatever meaning we can from the experience, and then release our attachment to it so we can move on. In January 2013, Fran was depressed. She was also frustrated because, after good progress throughout the previous summer and autumn, her efforts to lose weight had stalled. One night she complained to me of a blinding headache. I put it down to stress, poor sleep, or eye strain, and reassured her it would pass. Fran messaged me the next morning to confess.

Fran: i am angry and sad and mad and disgusted at myself.. last night the thing i didn't tell you was i ate a whole can of sweetened condensed milk.. that's why i had the raging headache.. all that sugar.. and i now weigh 154.4.. the last 2 weeks of no weight loss even though i was doing all the right things got to me.. i feel afraid that i will just start binging again.. disgusted with no results.. and feeling like nothing works.. why do it if it doesn't work.. i could just eat what i want instead of what's good for me.. why bother.. i don't know anything else i could do better..

Martin: You stumbled, Fran. You get to stumble sometimes. And you get to pick yourself up again.

I persuaded her to call me. She wasn't very communicative, but we continued our conversation. I suggested she used our mantra to process what was happening for her.

Fran: i guess the end of the world didn't happen.. it was just a hiccup.. a hiccup i had to have, to show me some things.. i really felt shitty last night.. my body responded to the sugar and carbs violently.. it would be good for me to remember that.. so there was some good that came of it.. i should journal about it..

Martin: Journaling would be good. This is what you do. You work with whatever you have. There is nothing that happens that we cannot learn from. Feel it. Claim it as your own, without blaming it on someone or something else. (You have done those two steps already.) Love it (accept and love yourself in this moment of awareness, which includes journaling it, working with it). Then let it go.

Fran: i'm exhausted.. i will exercise now.. my eyes feel heavy.. i will like this.. i will exercise.. even though i don't feel like it..

Martin: What you are feeling and going through is important. I hope I don't come across as making light of it in any way. I hope to help you see things as less black than they appear when you are in the middle of it all.

Fran: i am glad you don't overreact.. that would make me feel worse..

Care but Don't Crowd. Share but Don't Pollute.

This is a mantra of trust. "Care but don't crowd" reminds me to be there for Fran when she needs me, but not to nag her to tell me how she is doing, or pester her for attention. She deserves and needs her own space. "Share but don't pollute" is no less important. We are friends and I value her insight and support. I feel safe sharing my thoughts, experiences, and problems with her, but it is important not to share simply for the sake of it, or where doing so would drain her of energy she needs to keep herself well. I don't always get the balance right, but we trust each other enough for Fran to let me know if I am overburdening her.

Open Hands. Open Arms. Open Heart.

This important principle reminds us not to hold too tightly to people, relationships, and situations. Healthy things grow, and to grow is to change. In the time we have known each other Fran has moved from mania to depression and out again. She has grown in self-awareness, and developed tools for looking after herself. I have learned a great deal about what it is like for someone living with illness, and how to respond to Fran's needs and the needs of others. At times Fran needs me close beside her, at other times she needs space to grow independently.

"Open hands" recognises that change is natural, healthy, and necessary. It gives us permission to grow without feeling guilty or restricted. Imagine holding a small bird in the palm of your hand. It feels safe, protected, and cared for, but it is free to move, to grow, and even to fly away. "Open arms" reminds us that, no matter what happens, we will always welcome each other back as friends. "Open heart" connects our friendship to our wider network of relationships with other friends, family, and the people we encounter in our lives.

The Roles of a Friend

No matter who we are, we all assume various roles in our relationships with others. At different times, Fran and I have used a variety of labels to clarify our respective roles. These include friend, best friend, listener, confidant, teacher, balancer, haven, gate-keeper, and advocate. The three most fundamental are listener, balancer, and haven.

Being a Good Listener

Being a good listener is a very specific skill; knowing a person well and caring about them does not necessarily make the role easier. Four key points help me focus on what is important.

- Don't interrupt.
- Remember it's their story, not yours.
- Save your judgments for later.
- Don't try to fix everything.

Don't Interrupt

It is hard to listen to someone in distress—especially a friend or loved one—without offering comments, questions, suggestions, or potential fixes. Nevertheless, your friend needs to feel able to share without being interrupted or pressured to find a solution. This doesn't mean you must listen in complete silence, but resist the temptation to interject or influence the story. Small supportive comments will help things along, and occasionally echoing back what your friend has been saying will reassure both of you that the message is getting across. Ask for clarification if you do not understand, but do not pester for details. Allow your friend to share what they are ready to share.

Fran's thoughts sometimes flow so rapidly that she struggles to express them coherently. She hates me interrupting because it breaks her concentration; she finds it almost impossible to pick up the thread afterwards. This was hard for me in our early days. I found the frequent admonitions to "Just let me finish!" frustrating. I was interested in what she had to say, but often felt I was missing the opportunity to contribute ideas of my own or explore hers. If I pushed her, she would lose track and become irritated. Our tempers sometimes got the better of us, but gradually we learned to work together. These days, Fran lets me know if she is having trouble marshalling her thoughts, and I allow her to finish what she is saying before taking my turn. I still catch myself talking when I should be listening, but I am better at it than I used to be.

It's Their Story, Not Yours

If we have had similar experiences it is tempting to share. ("Oh, I know just how you feel. That happened to me.") We want to show we understand what our friend is going through, but the ways in which we were affected, how we responded, and the lessons we learned—or failed to learn—are part of our life story not theirs. No matter how well-meant, our recollections and advice are likely to be neither relevant nor helpful. We are also shifting the focus away from our friend, who might imagine we value their story less than we do our own. On the other hand, you may feel at a disadvantage if you have no similar experiences to draw on. I am fortunate to have known no major traumas in my life, and used to imagine this prevented me from connecting with people whose life stories were complex or traumatic. My friendship with Fran has taught me that whilst shared experiences can be useful, they are less important than a willingness to hold oneself open and honest. I no longer feel the need to apologise for the lack of trauma in my life.

Save Your Judgments for Later

Most of us like to believe we can listen to our friends without judging them, but there is a difference between forming an opinion (judgment) and imposing it on someone else. The former is healthy and necessary; the latter is, generally, unhelpful. Our opinions are based on our personal scales of goodness, rightness, or usefulness; if your friend trusts you then these scales are part of the person they trust. What counts is how you handle your opinions. You have a responsibility to voice your concerns if you believe your friend's situation or behaviour places them in danger. If the risk is serious or imminent it may be necessary to tell others; perhaps your friend's doctor, psychiatrist, hospital, or the police. We describe just such a situation in chapter 9. Otherwise, save your opinions for later, rather than interrupting what your friend is telling you. Note the beliefs that underlie your judgments. They tend to say more about you than they do your friend.

Don't Try to Fix Everything

This is the one I find hardest to put into practice! I have a tendency to suggest fixes for whatever seems to be wrong or broken. Fran will often ask for assistance, and I am happy to help if I can, but I need to remind myself that it is not my responsibility to resolve everything for her. To think otherwise would be unhealthy and disempowering for Fran. To focus only on what seems broken also robs her of the opportunity to simply talk through what is on her mind. Unless your friend specifically asks for assistance, assume that what they need right now is someone to listen. Better still, ask what your friend needs.

Being a Balancer

When Fran is in mania everything appears black or white to her. People are either angels or devils. Everyone loves her or everyone hates her. If things are going well, the universe is on her side and she is heedless of normal checks, precautions, and concerns. If something goes wrong, the whole world is against her. Depression skews her thinking heavily towards the dark. She loses track of even small successes and forgets that someone said something kind or was helpful. Things have always been as bleak and hopeless as they seem to be in that moment, and always will be. It is part of my balancing role to notice such unhealthy patterns, bring them to Fran's attention, and gently counter them. I first acknowledge that her thoughts and feelings are real to her. If I am unsure how factually accurate they are (did so–and–so really say or do what Fran is telling me they did?) I might try and draw out further details, or check Fran's story against other evidence. I then offer Fran my own interpretation—not necessarily as the truth, but as an alternative which might not have occurred to her. I am not always successful, but over time, this approach has helped shift Fran towards a more balanced way of thinking.

Being a Haven

The most important role you can fill is that of someone your friend can rely on, feel safe with, and trust to be always there. Fran has friends "who are designated to be the string of my balloon." We keep her grounded in times of mania, and prevent her from sinking too deeply when she is in depression. It is a cornerstone of our friendship that I am available for Fran no matter what is happening. We have spent many hours together when she has felt depressed, manic, anxious, afraid, or suicidal. There is little I can do to help on a practical level, but I can listen and talk with her. Above all, I can simply be there so that she knows she is not alone. Fran has written of this aspect of our friendship.

> [Marty] didn't try to change me. He didn't try to fix me. He was simply there, listening, being a friend. He believed in me when I couldn't believe in myself. One thing he said was that he wouldn't go away no matter what I said or did. That enabled me to share freely with him. Without that safe container it's much harder to share with people because boundaries are unclear.

Playing for the Team

I care deeply about Fran, but there are limits to my expertise, abilities, energy, and responsibilities. There are times when she needs help or support that I am ill-equipped or unable to provide. When that happens, it is important for me to remember I am not on my own; I am one member of a team of people involved in Fran's care. This is especially important in any sort of crisis when I might need to engage others, either to help assess the situation, or to intervene directly. The same applies to you and your friend, although details will differ.

Team Frannie

Fran's team includes close friends, her psychiatrist and doctor, various therapists, a care coordinator, and an Independent Support Services worker (homemaker). Your friend may have less professional support, but there will likely be a doctor, a few trusted friends, and perhaps also family members. Do you know who is on your friend's team? If not, take time to find out. In addition to the practical benefits, talking about the people involved in your friend's care, and their different roles, will help you both feel connected to something bigger than the two of you.

Don't Be Shy

Make the effort to introduce yourself to some of the people in your friend's support team. It is not necessary to become friends with them all—there may be practical or professional limits to the degree of contact possible—but it is reassuring to know who people are, and how you would contact them if necessary. Early in our relationship I exchanged details with several of Fran's close friends, as well as key support professionals. These details included postal address, e-mail addresses, telephone numbers (landline and mobile), and social media accounts. A more formal list of emergency contacts is built into Fran's wellness plan. I recommend also keeping some crisis line numbers to hand, such as the Samaritans (UK and Ireland), or the National Suicide

Prevention Lifeline (US). Befrienders Worldwide maintains a directory of international helplines. Details of these and other organisations—correct at time of going to press—are included in the appendix.

Team Marty

Remember that your friend is not the only one who needs support—you do too! I am fortunate in having a strong support team in my wife, immediate family, and network of friends. I am also a member of several online groups for friends and relatives of people living with mental illness. We talk more about self-care in chapter 7.

Growth and Change

It would be wrong to give the impression we are in a stable, fixed pattern in which we always know what to do and nothing ever goes wrong. There is little stable or fixed about living with mental illness or caring for someone who does. Our friendship grows as we face the challenges of our long-distance, mutually supportive relationship. Fran's health is inherently variable. Depression, mania, fatigue, and pain fluctuate—sometimes together, sometimes independently—and affect us in different ways. Her love of travel is a further challenge. It limits our ability to keep in touch, and can threaten Fran's health directly as she moves beyond her established routines and supports.

Our Natural Growth as Friends

Despite living on opposite sides of the Atlantic, we spend a considerable amount of time in each other's company. This has naturally built trust and respect, but disagreements are not uncommon. We have learned to deal with them promptly, recognising that our friendship is more important than whatever might have gone wrong between us. After two years as friends, the opportunity to meet face-to-face for the first time was a watershed. We were a little nervous, but confident we would relate as easily in each other's presence as we did online. We were not disappointed. It added to our shared experience without significantly changing our standing as friends.

Petty squabbles are one thing, but we also wrestle with deeper issues. Codependency is a psychological term for a situation in which someone gains satisfaction from another person being dependent on them. Perhaps surprisingly, both people may resist changing the situation, because each is subtly addicted to what is going on. It can develop in any relationship, but is a particular risk where one person is addicted, or incapacitated by illness in some way. In these circumstances, the other individual can become unhealthily attached to their role as caregiver. The first suspicion of codependency arose several months into our friendship. Fran felt she was relying too much on my support, and suggested we give each other some space. "I have needed you to be exactly as you have been so I could lean on you," she said. "And now I need you to be even more. To stand beside me."

I understood what she was saying, but her words triggered powerful feelings of loss and abandonment in me. It felt as though Fran wanted to end our friendship altogether, although I knew that was not true. It took a while to realise that my emotional reaction had little to do with us at all. It was part of my personal baggage from previous relationships. Recognising this enabled me to talk things through with Fran, who had been disconcerted by my reaction. Such feelings still arise from time to time, usually when Fran is doing relatively well and has less need of my support. It is a testimony to the strength of our friendship that we feel safe sharing and exploring our insecurities when they arise.

Wellness and Illness

The episodic nature of bipolar disorder has both positive and negative implications. During an episode of either mania or depression it is reassuring to know—though Fran may struggle to believe it at the time—that with appropriate care and treatment she will come through the other side. On the other hand, there is no cure, and no matter how vigilant she is Fran cannot rule out further episodes. Her realistic aim is to manage her condition as effectively as possible. When she is well enough, Fran turns her attention and energies outwards. She catches up with friends and resumes favourite activities; going to the cinema, theatre, and art galleries; walking about town and on the beach; and attending ice hockey and baseball games. She is also able to focus on personal projects such as homemaking and planning future vacations. She generally needs less from me in terms of practical support, and we spend less time together, though we continue to connect almost every day. My role shifts from actively providing support to ongoing vigilance.

Bipolar disorder is particularly unforgiving of complacency. When stable, Fran can let down her guard a little whilst I keep watch for potential triggers and red flag behaviours that might herald the onset of depression or mania. It can be difficult for me to adjust, but I remind myself that we are friends not because Fran is ill, but because we care about each other. Good or bad, well or unwell, we share whatever is going on in our lives. There are periods of darkness and struggle, but there are plenty of good times too. We watch movies and listen to music together. We meditate, read books, and encourage each other in our efforts to lose weight. These simple pleasures cement our friendship. They are as important as—and contribute to—our ability to navigate the challenges of a life lived with illness.

At Home and Away

My wife and I holiday in the UK two or three times a year. Fran loves to travel and takes trips within the US and abroad whenever her health and finances allow. No matter which of us is away from home, it is generally more difficult for us to stay in touch. The issues are mostly technical, but if Fran changes time zone it can also be hard to schedule times when we are both available to connect. We rely a great deal on instant messaging, and might manage to talk no more than briefly every few days. Video calls tend to be expensive or unworkable. The disruption can be extremely frustrating, and means I am unable to support Fran as effectively as usual. Nevertheless, we value the opportunities travel affords. Never having journeyed outside the UK, my knowledge of the world has been greatly expanded by accompanying Fran as her virtual travel buddy. Being less in touch also helps counter codependency, and fosters trust in both ourselves and our relationship. I wrote the following in my diary before Fran visited Spain with a friend. It was the first time she had travelled abroad since we met.

> Fran sees it working out that she will message me in the morning and in the evening, and maybe occasionally during the day. She wants to test how well she can handle letting go of most of her normal structures, including contact with me. She says this trip is about trusting herself. I was surprised at her setting aside so much of her routine all at once, but I can see what a leap of faith it is. I told her I won't worry, because I trust that she will be OK, and I trust her to tell me if she isn't. Likewise, she gets to trust that I will be OK, that I will deal with whatever I have to deal with while she is away.

Travel can pose significant risks to people living with bipolar disorder. The disruption in routines and sleeping patterns (exacerbated by changes in time zone) and the excitement of new experiences can trip some people into mania. Fran's ten-day trip to Spain left her physically and mentally exhausted, but passed with no lasting impact. A summer tour of Europe with her parents proved a far greater challenge. Fran knew it would not be easy ("Traveling in Europe with your 80-year-old German mother and her husband for three-and-a-half months is not for the faint of heart") but it proved far more demanding than we had anticipated. With phone contact limited to short calls often days apart, it was hard for me to gauge Fran's physical, mental, and emotional condition. For her part, Fran found it impossible to maintain healthy habits, routines, and behaviours. Despite these difficulties—and some very real risks—the experience was ultimately rewarding. As we describe in chapter 9, Fran learned she could handle difficult situations far from home and her usual support systems, with little knowledge of the local language. I learned to pay close attention to small shifts in her language and behaviour, how to book hotel accommodation for three people traveling in distant lands, and how to direct them to their destination using online map and routing services, satellite navigation, and instant messaging. We learned we could trust each other in times of crisis, and that the approaches we had established in easier times still worked when there was little else to rely on.

Summary

In this chapter we have looked at the qualities we believe are crucial to our success as friends, and some of the principles that guide us. We have talked about three key roles of a supportive friend: being a good listener, being a balancer, and being a haven. We have also touched on the importance of being part of a wider support team rather than trying to go it alone. Our relationship is not static but is continually evolving. It deepens over time as any healthy friendship does, but also changes according to the phases of Fran's illness, and whether we are at home or on vacation. In the next chapter we look at what illness means, the diagnostic labels of Fran's illnesses, their symptoms, and how they affect her day-to-day life.

2. The Illness Experience: Understanding Your Friend's Diagnosis and Symptoms

i am full of fatigue, pain, and happiness..
it's good to be alive..
—Fran Houston

"What is Bipolar Disorder?"

The term "bipolar disorder" covers a wide range of symptoms. Reflecting this, people are sometimes given a more specific diagnosis such as bipolar I (type one bipolar disorder), bipolar II (type two), rapid cycling, or cyclothymic disorder (cyclothymia). We look at the different types later in this chapter, but in simple terms bipolar disorder—also known as manic-depressive illness or manic depression—is a disorder of the brain that manifests as abnormal levels of mood and energy. We all experiences life's ups and downs, and it can be difficult to distinguish between the extremes of the normal range and the early or mild stages of a bipolar episode. As well as taking stabilising measures, which may include prescribed medication and therapies, it is vital for people living with bipolar disorder to monitor their mood and behaviour for any signs they are straying into mania or depression. Vigilance requires considerable discipline, focus, and energy; it can frustrate and exhaust both the person with illness and those who care for them. It is, nevertheless, necessary and worthwhile. Depression and mania are severely debilitating and may even threaten life itself.

The Causes of Bipolar Disorder
Whilst there seems to be no single cause of bipolar disorder, certain factors may increase the likelihood of developing the condition.

Chemical Imbalance

The mood swings of bipolar disorder are thought to be related to imbalances in the concentration of brain chemicals known as neurotransmitters. These chemicals carry messages from one neuron (nerve cell) to the next. Mania may be associated with higher than normal levels of transmitters such as norepinephrine; depression may be the result of levels being too low. Other neurotransmitters may be involved, including serotonin and dopamine.

Genetic Factors

Bipolar disorder tends to run in families. Having parents, brothers, or sisters with the condition means you are statistically more likely to develop it yourself, but you are by no means certain to do so. A genetic predisposition may increase the chances of other factors triggering bipolar episodes.

Triggers

Bipolar disorder often appears following a period of extreme stress. The nature of the stress seems relatively unimportant, and the event may trigger an episode of either mania or depression. If manic, the person may receive a relatively prompt diagnosis of bipolar disorder and commence appropriate treatment. If the initial episode is depression, it might be months—or even years—before it becomes clear that the person has bipolar disorder, rather than major depression (sometimes called unipolar disorder). Some antidepressant medications are implicated in triggering mania in certain cases. The so-called "kindling hypothesis" suggests that whilst it may take a major stress event to trigger an initial bipolar episode, future episodes may be triggered by progressively smaller challenges, until they recur without obvious external triggers. This theory (which originally arose from studies into epilepsy) does not account for the experiences of every person with bipolar.

Blame and Responsibility

Fran no longer blames herself for being ill, as there may have been genetic and other contributory factors over which she had little or no control. She nevertheless accepts responsibility for actions that may have precipitated bipolar disorder, such as pushing herself to extremes in her engineering career.

> I loved my work.. adored it.. was addicted to it.. I worked way too hard.. record was 110 hours in one week.. I never ever took lunch.. I smoked because that was the only way to get a break..

Things are not always clear-cut, however. Workaholism—the drive to overstretch oneself—may have its own predisposing factors and triggers. Fran's first episode of mania could have been triggered by the medications prescribed for her initial depression. A later manic episode coincided with, and was probably triggered by, a period of intense exertion and focus as she worked on her first book. Whatever caused her conditions, Fran works hard to become, and to remain, as well as possible. "I am not at fault for having illness," she says. "But I am responsible for caring for myself."

Experience and Understanding

Our attitudes towards illness and the ill are influenced by our experiences, as well as our broader values and beliefs. These are intensely personal. No matter how logical your approach seems to be, remember that others may feel differently about what it means to be ill, and how best to respond to the situation. If you are unsure of your friend's take on illness, ask. My perspective differed significantly from Fran's when we met, which is unsurprising given our vastly different backgrounds. Acknowledging and respecting those differences allows us to talk honestly about what is going on for Fran when she is unwell.

Martin's Experience of Illness

My father had chronic rheumatoid arthritis throughout his adult life. My memories are of a man progressively crippled by disease who refused to let it affect him more than absolutely necessary. He died when I was eighteen years old from infections his body was unable to fight after decades on oral steroids. My mother once asked me if I had resented the limitations his disability imposed on our family. The question astounded me. It had never occurred to me to think like that.

In my early twenties, I developed dermatitis on my hands and arms. It was painful and inconvenient, but I accepted it as something over which I had little control. It eventually cleared and has not returned. A few years later, I was hospitalized following an episode of acute abdominal pain and bleeding. The condition responded to anti-inflammatory medication, which I took preventatively for two years afterwards. I recall attending an outpatient appointment to learn the results of some diagnostic tests. I was prepared to discover I had experienced either a nasty but limited inflammation, or the first visitation of some serious, perhaps life-threatening, condition. The results were inconclusive, and the doctors decided further tests would not be performed unless the condition reoccurred. I remember feeling cheated. Even a serious diagnosis seemed preferable to doubt and uncertainty. Fortunately, the condition never troubled me significantly again.

Ten years later, a friend developed multiple sclerosis. I knew little of the disease, and never took the trouble to ask or research what it meant. My friend spoke pragmatically of the impact it would have on her life, imagining and planning for a gradual physical deterioration. The illness advanced far more rapidly than anyone anticipated. I watched helplessly as the woman I had known was overwhelmed by disease, despair, and grief. The depth of her need terrified me. I wrote to her every day for what turned out to be the last two years of her life, but never once picked up the telephone. I visited her home only once, after her death, to attend a memorial ceremony.

36

Looking back, I see I squandered many opportunities to develop a compassionate understanding of illness and its impact. My stoic attitude helped me deal with my own ill health, but left me incapable of responding with compassion to the needs of others. I mistakenly believed that caring for someone meant making their pain and hurt go away. It would be many years before I learned to open my heart and simply be there for those I care about. I am still learning.

Fran's Experience of Illness

I was a melancholic child. My mom sometimes called me Mona Lisa. I was a late bloomer and quite shy, although I played the piano, flute, and guitar. I was industrious, but high school was hard for me socially and I became bulimic as a way of coping. After high school, I fell into a cult. That sounds bad but it provided structure, community, and purpose. I was in the cult seven years until I met my husband. I got into engineering school, which I excelled at and graduated with honors. But my husband was abusive and I left him after seven years. By then I had a successful engineering career. I was also a workaholic and an alcoholic. I moved to Maine. My new partner and I built a home together, and raised three daughters. We had a good life. Then I got sick.

I was diagnosed with major depression in 1994. Following that, chronic fatigue syndrome and fibromyalgia crept in. I spent over 10,000 dollars on conventional and alternative medicine, but nothing worked. I asked my partner for more commitment. He declined and we broke up. I was devastated and became manic and exhausted. I lived alone in a cabin in the woods for a year to sort myself out, and then moved to an island. I wasn't diagnosed with bipolar until 2004, so for ten years I was treated with antidepressants. It is not good to treat bipolarists with antidepressants because it worsens their symptoms. For ten years, I was up and down, as my meds would work and then not work.

In the fall of 2010, I was on the mood stabilizer topiramate (Topamax) and an antidepressant. Looking back, I can see how my behavior was starting to ramp up to a full blown manic episode in the summer of 2011. Mania felt great. I was creative, fun, excited about living. I wasn't aware of my sickness until people started behaving differently towards me. I became aggressive and belligerent and people didn't know what to do with me. Some friends played hardball with me in a kind, direct way. Many others were mean and judgmental, or ignored me, and of course, I didn't understand at all. I did not realise how sick I was. In August 2011, I was prescribed risperidone (Risperdal). It had an immediate effect on my mania but that fall and winter brought the deepest suicidal depression I had ever experienced. My psychiatrist and I discussed putting me on lithium. I was afraid of the side effects but wanted to try it because it can work wonders with suicidal thinking. I started lithium in March 2012, and have been relatively stable since. It took a long time but I have accepted there is no cure for my illnesses and finally that gives me peace and grace. I have ups and downs of course. Marty and I have to be vigilant, but when I experience slight mania, I can get back to solid ground relatively quickly.

Other people are so important. Some are kind and caring. They help me and teach me about compassion for others. Steady, positive and life-affirming support is crucial. I have made so many bad choices. Being able to talk about options and choose the best ones means so much to me. When you have a broken mind, it helps to check things out with others who care. Marty is good for me because he sees me and my illness as separate things. When I am down in the dirt, he gets down in the dirt with me. Meditation helps. Firm kindness works best. We are all people, both the ill ones and the well ones. A chain is only as strong as its weakest link. A community is only as strong as its most vulnerable.

Labels of Illness

In this section, we examine the diagnostic criteria for a range of conditions: chronic fatigue syndrome, fibromyalgia, major depression, mania and hypomania, and bipolar disorder. It is not possible to cover these in detail or describe other illnesses, but there is a wealth of published information available. We encourage you to read as widely as possible on topics relevant to your friend's diagnosed condition.

What the Labels Mean and Don't Mean

Diagnostic labels are useful if they aid understanding and help target appropriate treatment, but they say very little about the person who carries them. As Fran puts it, "labels help me identify what is going on, but they are not me." Before we look at the labels themselves, it is important to understand what it means to have one or more of them applied to you. If you are diagnosed with a medical condition—bipolar disorder, for example—it does not mean that your doctor has discovered something called bipolar disorder lurking inside you. It means you have presented with a pattern of symptoms and behaviours that, in the clinician's opinion, match the currently accepted criteria for that condition. This might seem a subtle distinction, but it is an important one; the definitions of many illnesses, including mental disorders, are periodically revised.

The Diagnostic and Statistical Manual of Mental Disorders (DSM) and the International Statistical Classification of Diseases and Related Health Problems (ICD) are two collections of such definitions. They are intended for clinicians, rather than patients or the general public, but they affect us all. In the same way that law books define the crimes with which we may be charged, works such as these define the medical conditions with which we may be diagnosed. Needless to say, most of us are not clinically trained, and do not sleep with copies of the DSM or the ICD under our pillows. If we hear someone is bipolar, schizophrenic, or has chronic fatigue, we do not immediately head to the library, search the Internet, or order a copy of the latest diagnostic guide. Unless we have personal experience to help us, we are likely to base our interpretations on whatever we have previously heard, read, or otherwise picked up. This is fine, so long as we are open to expanding our awareness, but mental illness carries associations that are often far from wholesome, and these need to be challenged. "Crazy," "psycho," and "malingerer" are labels too.

The DSM and the ICD

Now in its fifth edition and referred to as the DSM-5, the *Diagnostic and Statistical Manual of Mental Disorders* (2013) is published by the American Psychiatric Association. It is used by doctors and researchers to define and classify mental disorders, primarily in the United States, but also in other countries. The previous edition (DSM-IV-TR) has been in widespread use since 2000, and is likely to remain the standard approach until the changes introduced in DSM-5 have established themselves.

In the absence of biological markers for mental illness, diagnosis is based on behavioural symptoms. To be diagnosed with a mental illness, your doctor must have determined you meet the criteria specific to that label. If you do not meet the criteria for type two bipolar disorder, for example, you do not have that condition. You may, however, satisfy the criteria for one or more other conditions. The DSM recognises that no definition can fully specify what is meant by a mental disorder, and that disorders are not necessarily clearly separated from one another (or from the condition of having no mental disorder). The DSM is not the only such classification. Published by the World Health Organization and currently in its 10th revision, the *International Statistical Classification of Diseases and Related Health Problems* (ICD-10) is widely used in Europe. Mental and behavioural disorders are covered in chapter V of the ICD.

Chronic Fatigue Syndrome

Uncertainty about the causes, nature, and even the existence of this condition has led to it being known by several names. The most common names are chronic fatigue syndrome (CFS), myalgic encephalomyelitis (ME), and the composite label CFS/ME. In 2015, The Institute of Medicine (now the National Academy of Medicine) suggested a new name, systemic exertion intolerance disease (SEID). This reflects the fact that many patients experience prolonged fatigue following physical or mental exertion. The label chronic fatigue syndrome highlights the condition's most obvious symptom, but gives no hint of others that may be no less disabling. These include flu-like symptoms, generalised pain and sensitivity to pressure, problems with thinking ("brain fog"), and psychological symptoms including anxiety and depression. The name is disliked by some, who feel it trivialises the condition's severity and complex nature. Fran refers to her condition by that name, however, and we use it throughout this book.

Fibromyalgia

The common diagnostic criteria for fibromyalgia were defined in 1990 by the American College of Rheumatology. The person must have experienced pain for at least three months affecting both sides of their body, both above and below their waist. The person must also experience pain in several of eighteen specific "tender points" distributed over the body. The number of points which are actively painful is not always considered crucial to the diagnosis.

Major Depression

There are a variety of diagnostic criteria for depression. The general criteria for what is called a major depressive episode are that the person has had a depressed mood and/or a lack of interest and pleasure for at least two weeks. The episode may be classed as mild, moderate, or severe, depending on the impact on the person's life and behaviour. Symptoms may include some or all of the following.

- Feeling depressed most of the day.
- Little interest or pleasure in usual activities.
- Significant changes in weight (either loss or gain).
- Changes in sleeping patterns (either too little or broken sleep, or more than usual).
- Difficulty performing tasks that are normally considered mundane or automatic.

- Tiredness (fatigue).
- Feeling worthless or guilty.
- Poor concentration or difficulty making decisions.
- Recurring thoughts about death, which may include suicidal thinking.

Two or more major depressive episodes are required to diagnose major depressive disorder.

Mania and Hypomania

Mania is a state of abnormally high or irritable mood, accompanied by unusually elevated energy levels. It can be thought of as the opposite of depression, and it forms the second pole in bipolar disorder. The term covers a wide spectrum of intensity. The milder traits associated with hypomania are not necessarily detrimental; there is a long-standing association between mania and creativity, drive and success. The key distinction between hypomania and full-blown mania is that in hypomania, the elevated mood and energy are kept under a degree of control. In hypomania, there is also an absence of psychotic components such as hallucinations and delusions.

The diagnostic criteria for a manic episode are that there is a distinct period, lasting at least a week (or any length of time if the person was hospitalised as a result) where the person's mood was abnormally and persistently high or irritable. Symptoms include some or all of the following.

- Feeling full of self-esteem or making grandiose plans.
- Less need for sleep than normal.
- Talking more, faster, or more relentlessly than usual.
- Racing flow of ideas.
- Being easily distracted.
- Increased activity (physically, socially, or sexually).
- Increased high-risk behaviour such as spending sprees, unwise business decisions or sexual excesses.

The diagnosis must rule out the possibility that these symptoms are the result of other causes such as drug abuse, side-effects of medication, or general medical conditions such as glandular imbalance. The elevated mood needs to be severe enough to significantly impair the person's ability to function (for example at work or in relationships with others) or to require hospitalisation. Although Fran has never exhibited psychotic symptoms, her episodes of abnormally elevated mood and energy meet the diagnostic criteria for mania.

Bipolar Disorder

Bipolar disorder is so-called because the person has, or has had, symptoms of both depression and mania (or hypomania). Bipolar disorder is commonly divided into three types (type one, type two, and cyclothymic disorder). The manic and depressive phases are generally responsive to medication, but successful treatment is likely to involve a multi-faceted approach including therapy, support, and education.

Bipolar I

The main criterion for diagnosing type one bipolar disorder is that there has been at least one episode of full blown mania. This will usually have lasted for at least a week; probably longer. There may or may not have been an episode of major depression. Alternatively, there may be episodes of mania and depression that cycle rapidly, perhaps even daily.

Bipolar II

A diagnosis of type two bipolar disorder requires there to have been recurring episodes of major depression accompanied by hypomania. Bipolar II may present as less extreme than bipolar I, but is no less dangerous.

Cyclothymic Disorder

This label is applied to conditions where there is a chronic cycling between hypomania and depression, but the criteria for bipolar I and II are not met.

Physical Symptoms

Fran's illnesses are complex and interrelated. We can separate their symptoms into physical effects (fatigue, pain, insomnia, and weight gain), and those which affect her mood and behaviour (mania, depression, and suicidal thinking).

Fatigue

It can be difficult to distinguish the lack of energy associated with depression from the symptoms of chronic fatigue and insomnia. Whatever the underlying cause, there are times when Fran struggles to accomplish what most of us consider routine or mundane tasks. These include preparing meals, taking a shower, household chores, and keeping on top of paperwork. Fatigue can be triggered by physical work, exercise, or changes in sleeping patterns and medication. Extreme emotions can also induce a fatigue crash. Fran can be focused and active, then find herself "wiped out" with little or no warning. She is unable to concentrate or function normally, and requires immediate bed rest. As beneficial as social engagements can be, for Fran they are physically and emotionally draining.

Pain

It is rare for Fran to be completely free from pain. In addition to the generalised pains characteristic of fibromyalgia and chronic fatigue, she experiences aches, soreness, and spasms in her neck, shoulder, and lower back. The latter may be related to earlier injuries—a fall in her teens while horse riding, and a skiing accident in her thirties—but some triggers are less than obvious. She once experienced debilitating headaches after consuming an entire tin of condensed milk. Fran takes oral analgesics as necessary. Acupuncture and osteopathy are also helpful. At other times, alcohol has been the only thing to provide significant relief, although that can lead to other problems.

Insomnia

Fran's sleeping has been poor for many years. She once spent a year living in the woods while deeply depressed, and slept up to twenty hours a day. She generally finds it hard to stay up beyond nine o'clock in the evening, but her sleep is fractured and unsatisfying. During periods of mania, she might stay awake until one or two o'clock in the morning, and then crash—mentally alert but physically exhausted. She might attempt to rest but be kept awake by her racing thoughts.

Weight Gain

There is a clear link between Fran's weight and some of her medications. From a previously stable baseline, her weight rose by ten pounds (4.5 kg) in five weeks when she began taking risperidone (Risperdal). It remained at this higher level for six months. At this point, Fran was prescribed lithium carbonate to counteract suicidal thinking. Weight gain is a well-documented side effect of lithium, and in less than three months she had put on another ten pounds. Fran was horrified at what was happening, and joined a weight control program. Within three months, she had reversed the increase which had been triggered by lithium by changing her patterns of eating and exercise. It took another six months to reverse the effects of risperidone. Maintaining her weight within healthy limits has been far from easy. There have been numerous setbacks as she has learned new ways of relating to her body, fitness, and diet. Her weight tends to rise sharply if she slips back into old patterns of behaviour, if she is stressed or unwell, or if her medication is changed.

Mood and Behaviour

Fran's illnesses affect her behaviour and mood in various ways; we focus here on mania, depression, and suicidal thinking.

Mania

Fran's experience of mania is not wholly negative; at times it has provided her with immense drive, energy, confidence, and creativity.

> My mania enables me to come out from the hole of depression, to find my voice, my passion. It is what has enabled my small measure of acclaim and success: my book, my appearances on TV and radio, and my poetry reading.

Mania can be intoxicating, both to the person experiencing it and those they encounter. Fran is naturally cautious, and it is unlikely we would have met at all if she had not been in mania. Active engagement in social media is one aspect of her manic personality. Another is her use of language. Our friendship triggered a creative response in her that was as unexpected as it was expansive.

> Two months ago, I met a poet from the United Kingdom online. Within days of that meeting, I found myself writing poetry! I had never appreciated poetry before then but suddenly there I was, writing it and receiving great feedback. My first live poetry reading was on August 1st [three months after we met]."

The poems that introduce each of the three parts of this book are from that period, but there were many more. Drawing directly on her life experience, most are free-flowing, unstructured, and peppered with puns and wordplay. She stopped writing altogether in the depression that followed her manic excess. The urge to write re-established itself in time, but in a completely different style. Her new poems were short, sometimes no more than two or three lines. Rather than describing her internal state, they portrayed the natural world around her.

But if some aspects of mania are benign and engaging, others are far less attractive. In the grip of mania, Fran clamoured for attention, and pushed her ideas at people whether they wanted to listen or not. She was capable of presenting herself with stunning clarity, but at other times her thoughts could be hard to follow. Such behaviour disturbs, worries, and alienates people. Some approached Fran with kindness, but from others there was mistrust and misunderstanding. Every negative reaction was acutely felt. The emotional pain of rejection far exceeded the physical pain of her other conditions.

> ... this.. is what.. i get.. un believable.. lies.. and un believable.. hatred.. and pain.. and knives.. inserted.. directly.. straight.. into my gut.. and heart.. twisted.. and turned..

She felt alone and very scared. She nevertheless resented any idea she should adapt to fit society's expectations of how she should behave. Mania drove her to speak the truth as she saw it. She was desperate to share with the world what life was like for her, so that other people would understand the plight of those who live with mental illness. There was something of the martyr about her zeal. She was capable of identifying herself with characters from history who had suffered for their causes, including Jesus Christ and Martin Luther King. Her grand project, Wild Hair, grew directly from this conviction. Although its practical agenda was never clearly defined, Fran envisioned Wild Hair as a non-profit organisation highlighting the condition of the ill, the homeless, and the dispossessed. These aims are not without merit, no matter how impractical they were for Fran to achieve. Fortunately, she reined the project in before too much money had been spent or committed.

Fran has not experienced a prolonged manic episode for several years, but we remain vigilant. Her wellness plan (described in chapter 3) lists behaviours that indicate she may be approaching mania.

- Talking really fast without regard for social norms.
- Not listening to others. Being argumentative, bossy or intense.
- Talking obsessively about suicide.
- Spending a lot of money.
- Needing very little sleep and having lots of energy.
- Drinking too much (more than a couple of glasses of wine or beer a day).
- Lots of hand waving, lip quivering, and mouthing.
- Obsessive writing and rhyming.

Depression

Despite its dangers, Fran has described depression as "my best friend, the one I was most comfortable with, a lifelong companion, a favorite blankie." The numbing weight of depression can appear to her a comfort and refuge, smothering the clamour of the outside world and its concerns. Depression brings Fran's focus and energy inwards. This can be debilitating, but she is relatively safer from harm—including self-harm—than when she is manic. That is not to say there is no risk, or that such an approach is appropriate for everyone. Fran's suicidal thinking is a danger at any time, and other people may be at particular risk when they are depressed. Everyone is different. Fran has generally received greater care and support during periods of depression. Most people have some idea—whether accurate or not—of what it feels like to be depressed, whereas mania can present as alien and bizarre. This is not the experience of everyone with bipolar disorder, however. Some people find mania makes them the proverbial life and soul of the party; though friends may desert them when they fall into depression and withdraw socially.

Despite Fran's assertion that "the dirt of depression has taught me to rest, and yields the most beautiful flowers," there are aspects of the condition that terrify her. This is especially true of the depression that follows mania, as happened some six months into our friendship. Fran had warned me the crash was coming, but I was completely unprepared for its impact on her and our relationship. Within weeks, she was unrecognisable as the creature of energy and vitality I had come to know. The period that followed was devastatingly bleak. She repeatedly asserted that she could see nothing beyond the end of that winter. It was not a suicidal impulse as such (although later I found out she regularly counted the pills in her stash). It was a simple and terrifying inability to see anything beyond her present situation. It took months for her to emerge from that darkness. I wrote the following letter to a mutual friend.

> Fran has come so very far. To have brought herself out of her depression, to have put herself onto lithium, to have got herself out and about with her walking and her bike rides so she is getting exercise and also meeting people again, to have worked at sorting out things with the house and to be getting her weight down again, and a handle on her finances. She staggers me on a daily basis. The guts and sheer bloody determination it takes. She has done it with our care and support, but she has done it. And it has led to her looking ahead into the future.

As with mania, we are vigilant for the return of depression. The following behaviours suggest Fran may be approaching a depressive episode.

- Not wanting to do anything.
- Talking of giving up. "It's not working."
- Not showering, brushing her teeth, or otherwise caring for her personal hygiene.

Suicidal Thinking

Suicidal thinking (sometimes called suicidal ideation) has been a part of Fran's life since childhood. Like most of her symptoms, it comes and goes in waves. It was a surprise to me to realise that there are different types of suicidal thinking. Some arise in response to what is going on in her life or how she is feeling. Others appear out of nowhere and seem to be symptoms of illness itself. Lithium has been successful in suppressing the latter, but other forms seem resistant to medication and have to be handled in other ways. We look at suicidal ideation in detail in chapter 7, where we also see how I support Fran when she is thinking about harming herself or wanting to die.

Summary

In this chapter, we looked at how experience shapes our understanding of illness, and examined the diagnostic labels for a number of conditions including chronic fatigue syndrome, fibromyalgia, depression, mania, and bipolar disorder. We have also seen how the symptoms can affect someone who lives with them on a day-to-day basis. In the next chapter, we look at the other side of the coin. We explore what wellness means, and some of the approaches Fran has found helpful. These include medication, therapy, mindfulness, and meditation.

3. The Way to Wellness: Treatments, Therapies, and Vigilance

be well.. deep well..
—Fran Houston

"When Will My Friend Get Better?"

Someone diagnosed with bipolar disorder is unlikely ever to be permanently cured, but that is not to say there is no hope. Each person, like each diagnosis, is unique. In our experience, it is certainly possible to recover from individual episodes of mania and depression. During an acute episode, the focus is on managing symptoms so your friend can return to a state of relative stability. Afterwards, the emphasis shifts to maintaining balance, and minimising the frequency and severity of future episodes. This is not an exact science. Each change in treatment—especially a change in medication or dosage—requires time to settle in before the benefits and side-effects can be assessed. It may take months, or even years, to find a treatment regime that works. Even then, there is no guarantee it will continue to be effective. Bear all this in mind if you ever feel frustrated at your friend's apparent lack of progress or improvement. Simply getting from one day to another can be a huge, and largely unrecognised, achievement. Be the person who recognises it.

Getting Well and Staying Well

In the last chapter we explored the symptoms Fran lives with day-to-day. Let's turn now to how she limits their impact, so as to live as fully and richly as possible. We discuss only medications, therapies, and other treatments Fran has used personally. These may not be directly relevant to your friend's situation. As Fran expresses it, "What works for me may not work for you, and vice versa. We need to find our own ways and make peace with them." It is also important to note that no strategy works forever. What we report as having worked for Fran in the past may not do so in the future. In the realm of chronic illness, wellness is a dynamic experience. We hope, nevertheless, to convey two important messages. The first is that there is no magic fix. Complex conditions such as bipolar disorder are likely to require multidisciplinary approaches including medication, therapies, and behavioural strategies. The second message is that it takes formidable commitment to stay as well as possible. It is not unreasonable to hope for dramatic improvements, but they can be a long time arriving, and may not last as long as you and your friend would hope. If so, it is not your friend's fault—nor is it yours.

The Nature of Wellness

We all want the best for the people we care about. If they are ill or hurting, we want them to get better. But for someone with chronic illness "getting better" is not like waiting for a broken arm to mend or an infection to clear. Wellness can never be taken for granted. It is neither a prize to be won nor a place of safety to be reached. It is more like a skill that can be developed, practiced, and refined. Medication has a role to play, but there is a lot more to it than remembering to take your tablets.

> For me the basics of wellness are nutrition, exercise, sleep, and hygiene. Those are non-negotiable. I start wherever I am and make the tiniest of shifts and changes, whatever I can handle at the time. It's as if your body/mind is a spaceship and you are creating the owner's manual. You are the only one who gets to make those choices. You can then share this manual with others who can support you in your process.

> Acceptance is critical. It was only when I came to utterly accept my illnesses and myself, stopped desperately looking

for fixes, and realized that there was nothing outside myself that would save me that my life began. I started being truly responsible and caring for myself.

There have been many things that have helped me and many things that have hurt me. I have also significantly hurt myself by my own thinking and actions. I learned that I could change that. I may not be able to be cured but I can stop making things worse. That was a revelation. I started being responsible for whatever I could, instead of blaming everything and everyone else for my problems: the doctor, the meds, friends, other people. I started owning my life.

Clinical Compliance

Also called adherence, compliance describes how closely a patient follows (is compliant with) medical advice. It can be tempting to stop taking medication if it causes unpleasant side effects, if it seems not to be working, or once symptoms have eased. It often takes time, however, for drugs to take effect, and it may be necessary to try several different treatments, individually or in combination, until a balance is found between the positive benefits and unwanted side effects. It is rare for Fran to miss a dose, and she consults with her doctor before stopping a course of medication or starting something new. When traveling, or if her routine is otherwise likely to be disturbed, she asks me to remind her to take her tablets on time. There is also a social aspect to compliance. People sometimes see unstable behaviour and incorrectly assume the person has stopped doing all he or she can to stay as well as possible. This happened to Fran and it hurt her deeply.

[Many people] were mad at me for apparently going off my meds during what was the most excruciating manic experience I have ever had. I can understand how people might think that, especially if they do not have experience of friends or family with mental illness, but it simply was not true. I have been on many different medications over the years, and have always been completely compliant in taking them. The truth is that no meds are perfect, and what I was taking simply stopped working for me. I saw my psychiatrist on a weekly basis, and kept all my other appointments. When my medication was changed by my psychiatrist my mania came back under control, though it was very difficult dealing with the transition and side effects, and the deep suicidal depression which came afterwards.

Bear this in mind if you are concerned that your friend might have stopped taking their medication, or accidentally missed a dose or two. There is a big difference between gently asking what is going on, and accusing your friend of careless or unhealthy behaviour.

Wellness and Fatigue

An acute episode of fatigue can debilitate Fran for days, if not weeks. With no specific treatment, she focuses on carefully monitoring her energy levels, and scheduling appointments and activities, in order to allow the necessary rest time. Not everyone understands the discipline this takes, or recognises that someone living with fatigue pays a high price for activities most take for granted.

> I rest a lot more than anyone realizes. People see me out and about or posting online and think I must be OK. I have to rest and get downtime after each outing. If I'm out for three hours then napping is a must. If I'm out for a day, the next day I rest.

Downtime is difficult enough to manage in Fran's home environment; it can be far harder when she is travelling. Pushing herself to continue without rest when her body is desperately fatigued also carries the risk of triggering mania.

Wellness and Pain

Fran is seldom completely free from pain. She has tried numerous treatments, mostly with limited success.

Medication to Minimise Pain

Ibuprofen, Naproxen, and Acetaminophen
Fran takes ibuprofen (Advil), naproxen (Aleve), and acetaminophen (Tylenol) for headaches and general aches and pains. They have little effect on the diffuse pain associated with chronic fatigue syndrome and fibromyalgia which varies in location and intensity.

Self-Medication with Alcohol
Whether we judge it wise or not, some people living with illness use alcohol to ease their symptoms. Fran knows it is an unhealthy habit when in excess, but admits to self-medicating during times of extreme fatigue and pain.

> The beer and wine I drink mostly at home is to assuage the intense pain, and to help overcome the fatigue which incapacitates me and makes me unable to speak clearly to others. Tylenol and Advil don't cut it. Alcohol in moderation is the only relief I have.

Fran also uses alcohol—and to a lesser extent has used nicotine—to stabilise her mood.

Therapies to Minimise Pain

Hypnotherapy
Fran has found hypnotherapy relieves her neck and shoulder pain, and also helped her establish healthy habits for sleeping and diet.

> I came to hypnotherapy for help with pain, insomnia, and weight loss. In the first session the intense pain in my neck

and shoulders disappeared, and has subsequently been much easier. Insomnia was a tougher issue, being that it is cyclic in nature. However, learning simple tips enabled me to gain better sleep. I am also better able to move through my emotions in relation to food. Rarely did I feel like I was doing anything in the sessions, but later I would find myself doing things effortlessly, creating habits where there had been none. Habits I had always wanted to develop.

Acupuncture, Osteopathy, Chiropractic, and Massage

These therapies reduce the impact of Fran's symptoms, especially pain and fatigue. All have been beneficial—"I need an acupuncture session to put me back together"—with massage and chiropractic proving the most effective.

I have arthritis in my neck, and my hips are out of alignment. Other parts shift to compensate and end up out of shape too. Wellness is about getting everything into alignment. I have gained so much from massage. My relationship to my body is substantially transformed, and my ability to manage fatigue, pain, and mood is much more consistent and resilient. My massage therapist identified some core issues, from the base of my spine up to my neck. That's work for chiropractic. Massage works with the muscles. Chiropractic works with the bones. My last chiropractor used an activator [a handheld instrument which delivers a jolt to the spine]. I liked it, and thought it was doing something. My new therapist is very different. He tells you what he is doing, so it's really interesting and engages my mind as well as my body.

BioMat

The Richway BioMat is an infrared and negative ion heating pad for which various healing effects are claimed. These include reduced stress, fatigue and anxiety; enhanced relaxation and sleep patterns; and the easing of pain, stiffness, and inflammation. Fran first tried the BioMat during an episode of mania when she was also experiencing severe pain and fatigue. She continues to use the device almost every day. It has not brought lasting relief, but she finds it relaxing and soothing.

Wellness and Insomnia

Fran has tried many medications, therapies, and strategies to relieve her insomnia. Of these, trazodone, hypnotherapy, and guided visualisations have proven the most effective.

Medication for Insomnia

Acetaminophen plus Diphenhydramine
Tylenol PM contains the general analgesic acetaminophen in combination with diphenhydramine hydrochloride, an antihistamine with sedative properties. Fran has taken it, with limited success, to counter night pain and insomnia.

Zolpidem
Fran has used the sedative zolpidem (Ambien), alone or in combination with Tylenol PM, to help with her sleeping. She finds it helpful, but less effective than trazodone. It is also addictive and she has found it hard when reducing her dose or stopping taking it altogether.

Trazodone
Trazodone hydrochloride (Pliva 433) is primarily used in the treatment of depression and anxiety, but in low doses it can be prescribed for insomnia. Fran learned of trazodone from a friend, and asked her doctor if it might relieve an especially severe episode of insomnia. It took a couple of weeks to begin working, but helps normalise Fran's sleeping to the extent that she wakes most mornings feeling rested and refreshed. She still has some poor nights, but prefers that to feeling sedated, as she had with other sleep medications.

Sleep Hygiene

Before discovering trazodone, Fran attended sleep hygiene classes. Each morning for six months she recorded when she went to bed, the times she woke, what medications she had taken, how much she had exercised, when she ate, and how much coffee, tea, water, and alcohol she had consumed. Her mood was generally stable, but she never once managed an uninterrupted night's sleep. Although no clear insights emerged, the exercise helped Fran to review her expectations. She realised she could function tolerably well with two or three short interruptions through the night. Three or more disrupted nights in a row left her prone to depression and feelings of hopelessness.

Guided Visualisations

Meditation and guided imagery have been helpful, especially in combination with trazodone. Fran uses these techniques before settling down to sleep, and if she wakes through the night. We look at these in more detail later in this chapter.

Wellness, Weight, and Body Image

Fran's weight, her body image, and her relationship to food are closely interrelated. They also interact with her mood and other symptoms. Illness makes it harder to maintain a healthy lifestyle, and weight gain is a common side effect of many medications used to treat mental disorders. When Fran is depressed, she finds it hard to motivate herself to exercise or eat well. Insomnia and fatigue leave her little energy to plan, shop for, or prepare healthy meals. It becomes tempting to rely on convenience and snack foods, which are high in calories and encourage overeating. Comfort eating—using food to provide temporary relief from her symptoms—and self-medication with alcohol only add to the calorie load. Weight gain is more than physically unhealthy. In her twenties Fran was actively bulimic.

Working to normalise her weight and eating can trigger old feelings of unworthiness, self-loathing, and failure. When on track towards her targets, she feels hopeful about her ability to make positive changes. At other times, her weight has plateaued for days or weeks at a time, and it is not always obvious why this happens. If she is already feeling low, the frustration of not understanding what her body is doing can cause her mood to plummet, making it hard for her to maintain healthy habits. This happened when Fran was traveling in Europe. She gained twenty pounds in six months, putting on almost all the weight she had lost in the previous year.

Fran has tried a number of diet, healthy eating, and weight loss strategies. No single approach has been completely successful, but each has contributed to Fran developing strategies of her own. When applied consistently, these allow her to counter the weight gain caused by her medication and work towards a healthier lifestyle.

Diet and Nutrition

Weight Loss Programmes

Weight Watchers and SparkPeople are diet and healthy living programmes which help people monitor the food and drink they consume. Weight Watchers uses a proprietary points system; SparkPeople tracks calories. Fran has found both programmes helpful in monitoring her eating, drinking, and exercise. Over a two year period, she has determined her personal calorie (SparkPeople) and point (Weight Watchers) thresholds, which differed from the ranges suggested by those programmes. Above these thresholds Fran gains weight; at or slightly below them, her weight is stable or reduces in a healthy and sustainable manner.

Daily Weight Chart

Body weight varies day-to-day by up to a couple of pounds (1 kg). By weighing each morning—rather than weekly—Fran is able to assess the underlying trend in her weight more easily, be that trend upward, downward, or static. She has learned a great deal about how her body functions, and her relationship to it. Recognising the noise in the signal allows her to see what is happening without attaching value judgments to the numbers (such as labelling down as good, up as bad). We have collected more than two years' worth of data. This helps when Fran is frustrated at her lack of progress, because I can point to times in the past where her weight stalled for a time and then began falling again. We can also identify patterns, such as the fact that Fran finds it harder to lose weight during the winter. She stays closer to home in poor weather and gets less exercise. She also tends to comfort eat to counter a tendency towards seasonal depression. Sharing her weight with me each day is protective, because Fran cannot hide any overindulgence for long.

Good Nutrition

It is impossible to overstate the importance of good nutrition to a person's health and wellness. With the support of her care coordinator and nutritionist she works to develop healthy attitudes and habits which will be sustainable in the long term. These support not only her physical health, but also her emotional and mental well-being. Fran's eligibility to receive Meals on Wheels assistance rests on her disabled status, which in turn is based on her clinical diagnoses. On one occasion, we feared the assistance might be withdrawn because she was relatively stable at the time she was reassessed. Her care coordinator supported her continued use of the service, and I wrote a letter expressing my opinion as caregiver.

> Having reliable access to healthy meals has had a very positive impact on Fran over the past two years, which may be hard to appreciate without a familiarity with her personal situation. Any sudden withdrawal of Meals on Wheels would be massively destabilising and potentially dangerous. We are especially concerned that periods of relative wellness might lead to her losing the service in the future, because Meals on Wheels itself is vital to Fran achieving and maintaining such stability.

Fran continues to receive home-delivered meals, but this could be withdrawn at any time. She works hard to develop skills and strategies to support herself nutritionally should that ever happen.

Exercise

Moderate exercise is often suggested for people with mental illness, especially depression. Nevertheless, it took weeks of gentle encouragement for Fran to start taking walks on the beach near her home as she emerged from depression following a prolonged episode of mania. She gradually extended her range until she was walking or cycling to local shops and to visit friends. It took longer for her to acknowledge it was helping to shift her mood.

As we noted in chapter 2, chronic fatigue syndrome is also known as systemic exertion intolerance disease (SEID), reflecting the fact that many people with the condition are particularly sensitive to exercise. Fibromyalgia also requires a graduated exercise programme to prevent what Fran terms the rubber band effect: a rebound crash of pain and fatigue. Soon after moving to the city, Fran took advantage of her local gym. She was aware of the dangers, but in her determination to lose weight, she pushed herself too hard. As she recalls, "I started out full throttle, lifting weights and riding bikes. I've always been an overachiever! After three weeks, I hit the wall big time. For a month after I was unable to do anything." She looked for gentler disciplines, and found a local exercise class designed for older adults. Its impact on her life has far exceeded her initial hopes of losing weight and improving her fitness.

Despite my pain and fatigue, I find the class to be not only doable, but enjoyable. It is critical for me to move, but do so in a way that does not exacerbate my illnesses. Any time I struggle, the instructor offers creative and custom solutions. The mental exercises we do help me to have more focus and resilience. At the end of each lesson we gather together for readings of inspiration. We all meld socially in a way that is mutually supportive, caring, and inspiring. In so many ways, it continues to change my life. I feel I've found my tribe.

Wellness and Mood

Depression, mania, and suicidal thinking are arguably the most dangerous of Fran's symptoms. She has used—and continues to use—a range of medications, therapies, and strategies to limit their impact. We focus here on treatments she has experienced during the time we have been friends.

Medication to Promote Mood Stability

Topiramate

Topiramate (Topamax) is used to treat seizures and migraine headaches, and as a mood stabiliser in the treatment of bipolar disorder. Unlike many of the drugs used in the treatment of mental illness, topiramate generally causes weight loss. It is sometimes prescribed to counter the weight gain caused by other medications. Fran rapidly lost weight when she started taking topiramate in 2005, although she gained it back later. She also recalls intense suicidal thinking in the early months. This reduced in time, but topiramate failed to manage her moods effectively. She stopped taking it early in 2012, when she was prescribed lithium carbonate.

Risperidone

Risperidone (Risperdal) is an antipsychotic which helps control the extreme emotions, thoughts, and behaviours associated with schizophrenia and bipolar disorder. Fran was prescribed risperidone in 2011 to counter an intense episode of mania that was not being controlled by topiramate alone. The initial side effects were overwhelming.

first week on Risperdal.. so very tired.. sleeping so much more.. can't wake up.. doing a lot less.. groggy.. sleepy eyed rubbing.. left swiss cheese in silverware drawer.. someone gave me a food care package which i promptly forgot about and left on the living room floor.. i am forgetting more than that too.. like who people are.. what we said..

Not trusting her own insights, Fran asked a few close friends what positive changes they had noticed. One friend focused on improvements in her mood and speech.

One aspect of the change I've seen is the way Fran is conversing. Her speech has less of an affected cadence to it. The sentences are less halting, and flow out in greater length with more complete ideas and insight. . . . I seem to sense an increased calmness. Not a total calmness, mind you, that would be alarming. But perhaps a more considered response in general. Maybe a little more empathy.

Another noticed significant changes in Fran's thinking and listening skills.

I think your logic and reasoning have been more controlled lately. You seem to be lashing out less, and you are definitely less paranoid. I think you are more willing to listen. Your language has more confidence, and your observations are more profound and open-minded.

Risperidone stabilised Fran's mood, but it also led to a dramatic increase in her weight, and she was keen to stop taking it as soon as it was safe to do so. This proved difficult, however, even when the dosage was lowered gradually. The main withdrawal effect was insomnia. The first attempt resulted in such poor sleep and disturbed mood that Fran was returned to her original dose of risperidone after five weeks. She tried again six months later. The withdrawal effects were the same, but this time she persevered. Her mood and sleeping finally stabilised after two or three months. Despite the difficulties, risperidone remains Fran's preferred medication if she begins experiencing symptoms of mania.

Lithium

Risperidone controlled the acute mania Fran experienced during 2011, but she became increasingly concerned about her suicidal thinking. Lithium has a long history as a mood stabiliser, and is reported to reduce thoughts of suicide and self-harm. Fran was nevertheless wary. Lithium has a number of potential side effects. It causes weight gain, but more seriously can become toxic if blood levels are not carefully controlled. We researched its side effects, toxicity, and effectiveness, and Fran discussed it at length with her psychiatrist. She was weaned off topiramate early in 2012, and began taking lithium a couple of months later. It has been a great success. Lithium suppressed her suicidal thinking rapidly and effectively. Fran is maintained on the lowest therapeutic dose, and has regular blood tests. Side effects have been minimal, but we remain vigilant for any indication of toxicity, such as dizziness, poor coordination, or blurred vision. As anticipated, Fran's weight began rising soon after starting lithium, but she took this as an incentive to examine her diet and take moderate exercise.

Self-Medication with Alcohol, Nicotine, and Food

Earlier in this chapter, we mentioned Fran's use of alcohol to dull the impact of pain. Drink also tempers the mental racing of mania, and buffers mixed episodes such as Fran experienced when traveling in Europe. Despite its undoubted effectiveness, Fran's claim to take alcohol only in moderation can be challenged. It certainly was challenged during a past episode of mania by people worried by her erratic language and behaviour. It is likely Fran underestimated the amount she was drinking at the time, but I rarely witnessed her visibly intoxicated, and her symptoms are open to misinterpretation. As Fran notes, "Mania in full flow can be confused with drunkenness, as can fatigue so acute that it can leave me slumped in a chair, or in a corner." Deserved or not, the slur of drunkenness caused her considerable problems and distress. She stopped drinking for a time, but found her symptoms intolerable.

> people's perception of me made me think twice.. made me hesitate.. i had two weeks of not drinking.. of intense excruciating pain.. of not being able to keep my eyes open.. of not being able to live any semblance of a life.. it is.. my only pain med.. the only thing that peps my sorry ass up..

Fran was also self-medicating with cigarettes during this period. She stopped smoking as soon as her mood was stabilised with prescribed medication, and reduced her drinking considerably. She did not smoke again until 2013 when it helped alleviate the stress of traveling in Europe with her elderly parents. She again ceased smoking once the crisis has passed. Comfort eating is another form of self-medication, which in Fran's words "superficially numbs and mutes the jagged edges of my feelings." Whatever form it takes—overindulgence in otherwise healthy meals or bingeing on junk food—comfort eating provides temporary relief at a high price: weight gain, guilt, and self-loathing.

Therapies to Promote Mood Stability

As Fran describes, "I've had a lot of therapy, and I've worked really hard at getting the principles of DBT, CBT, EFT, ACT, and numerous others. That bedrock of experience made coming to meditation, mindfulness, and guided imagery easier than if I had started out there, simply because my hamster wheel mind would not have been ready."

CBT and DBT

Cognitive Behavioural Therapy (CBT) and Dialectical Behaviour Therapy (DBT) are related techniques used to help people who are dealing with mood and behaviour disorders. CBT is based on the premise that becoming aware of our thinking, and where necessary replacing old patterns with newer and healthier ones, can improve how we feel and behave. DBT extends this to include acceptance and mindfulness, inviting us to be fully aware of the present moment and observe our feelings and situation without self-judgment. Fran tried both therapies during an episode of deep depression when she was also wracked with pain and fatigue. "I serviced myself well with CBT and DBT for two years to avoid hospitalization." She found DBT especially helpful and has continued working with acceptance and mindfulness in other contexts.

Acceptance and Commitment Therapy
ACT (usually pronounced as the word "act") emphasises forgiveness, acceptance, compassion, and living in the present moment. It is based on the idea that psychological suffering is caused by our efforts—whether conscious or unconscious—to avoid painful thoughts, feelings, and memories. ACT teaches techniques to change our relationship to those undesired experiences, reducing their impact and allowing us to focus on more positive things. Fran attended a ten week classroom-based course, and found it useful in working through a number of personal issues. I completed an online introduction to the principles of ACT so I could follow what Fran learned in class and help her practice it at home.

Neurofeedback Therapy
Reported to be effective in ADHD and epilepsy, neurofeedback therapy trains people to increase or decrease certain types of brain waves, in order to generate changes in their thinking, emotions, and behaviour. The therapist places recording electrodes on the head of the subject, who receives live cues (images and sound) to indicate whether his or her brain waves are within the desired range. Fran was given the opportunity to try neurofeedback therapy for ten weeks. She found it interesting and beneficial. Her sleeping became more consistent and she reported feeling generally calmer, more resilient, and more

present with what was happening in her life. "I don't get how neurofeedback works," she told me. "But it does."

Emotional Freedom Technique

Emotional Freedom Technique (EFT), sometimes known as tapping, is claimed to treat a number of psychological and physical issues including anger, grief, addiction, and depression. The technique involves tapping specific points on the face and body whilst acknowledging the issue using a specific form of words. For example, "Even though I have these feelings of anger, I deeply and completely love and accept myself." Fran was introduced to EFT by a friend who had recently qualified as a practitioner. She had some very positive experiences, as I recorded in my diary.

> The revelation which came to Fran during her EFT session today is that she needs to love *herself*, take care of *herself*, feed *herself* properly, etc. I was in tears as she told me, because in all the time I have known her, Fran has not seemed to care much for herself at all. This is a major shift, and part of my job will be to help her stay on that track.

Once the basic technique has been learned, EFT is meant to be self-administered. Fran found this difficult. "It's hard to do myself. I immerse myself in it, but can't quite get the insights." She nevertheless continued using it to explore issues such as low self-esteem.

> i want to see myself better than i have done.. i hear what marty says about my successes and inner beauty.. and i know some of that to be true.. but right now i feel fat.. i am EFTing around that to get better perspective and not feel so down on myself for being overweight.. because no matter my size i deserve to love myself..

Meditation and Mindfulness

In 2012, we learned of a free twenty-one day series of online meditations. Fran had read that meditation could benefit people living with depression and we decided to take the course together. Since that time we have completed online series led by various teachers, and meditate together most evenings. Fran begins every day with meditation, and has attended classes locally in both meditation and mindfulness. Mindfulness invites us to be more aware of our thoughts, emotions, and physical sensations in the present moment. Both techniques help Fran differentiate her own thoughts from those influenced by depression or mania, and see herself as separate from her illnesses.

> i love meditating.. paying attention to my breath or body or the mantras.. i feel it is helping me deepen the quality of my life and being.. the meditations and talks remind me of what health is and how to promote it.. the most useful thing has been the daily practice and the reminders of what's important..

There were times, however, when she became disappointed and frustrated because she was not making the progress she wanted.

> i don't know if i am missing something with meditation.. it seems to be just watching my breath.. it doesn't change anything.. i don't know that i'm any calmer..

With characteristic stubbornness, she persevered. She gradually learned to relinquish her need to "get somewhere already" and allow her experience of the moment to suffice.

> meditation still feels empty and boring.. there's nothing there.. but i am letting go of trying to get somewhere with it.. i'm not so pissed off any more.. i have acquiesced.. i have still not gotten to peace or joy.. but i am more accepting..

Meditation and mindfulness do not cure anything, but they improve Fran's ability to manage her symptoms. They allow her to step back from, and observe, old emotional and physical responses to events and situations in her life—including illness—without judging herself for them.

> meditation helps me to be mindful throughout the day.. i pay attention to my body more, am aware of it more than ever before.. and respect it.. i can adjust when i am off balance now..

Guided Visualisations

In the spring of 2014 Fran met with her psychiatrist and general practitioner. She was desperate for something to alleviate a severe episode of insomnia and fatigue, and hoped to be offered screening tests or medication. Instead, she was prescribed a series of guided imagery podcasts. Fran was disgusted. The recordings seemed no more likely to help than the alternative approaches her friends were suggesting.

> A friend called this morning.. says she has a cure.. something about pendulums.. one's bringing kava tea.. another wants me in essential oils.. Now my doctors give me guided imagery..

Despite her misgivings Fran started listening to the podcasts. Each comprised a guided imagery meditation lasting twenty-five minutes, followed by twenty-five to thirty minutes of positive affirmations. There was little effect at first but she persisted, determined to prove her doctors wrong.

> I've been listening to the guided imagery for over a month now.. 2–3 times a day.. supposedly you don't really have to listen for them to be effective.. thing is, the affirmations and positive thinking just seem to piss me off because my life isn't like what is being said.. i don't have a clue how to get

there.. these are what my doctor recommended instead of tests like thyroid or hormones which is what i asked for..

In time, she found the podcasts integrated well with her meditation and mindfulness practice. Collectively, these techniques have had a pronounced influence on her stability, mood, and motivation.

i've learned it's not about getting anywhere.. it's about being exactly where you are.. you need not DO anything.. it's about being with yourself just as you are.. wild thoughts crazy thoughts suicidal thoughts depressed thoughts all get to be there.. they are simply clouds in the sky.. when i first started i had no space between my thoughts.. then a baby bit of space.. now.. two years later i am actually able to "be" in the moment instead of the old hamster wheel mentality.. my illness is not gone.. but i've found tools to help me manage..

The Need for Vigilance

No matter how effective Fran's medications are, and no matter how diligently she works at her therapies and self-care, wellness can never be taken for granted. If life is a journey, illness is part of the landscape through which Fran travels. It is easy for her to inadvertently find herself in regions of mania, depression, insomnia, pain, or fatigue. Staying well requires Fran—and those who care for her—to be constantly vigilant. It is part of my role as her friend to watch for behaviours and situations which suggest she is becoming unwell. Fran has developed a number of vigilance strategies in collaboration with her professional support team. Central to these are her personal care manual and wellness plan. An example of each is included in the appendix.

Personal Care Manual

Fran's personal care manual is a living document that she updates from time to time. It captures her personal life goal ("To create a warm loving home—in my body, in my mind, in my dwelling, in my travels—by living and eating healthfully and choicefully.") and key aspects of her self-care. In Fran's words, "My care manual lists things that are good for me, whether I am manic or depressed or pained or fatigued or well. When I stop doing these things it means I am not well and need support and encouragement to return to these basics."

Wellness Plan

Fran's wellness plan is designed for friends, family, and others she trusts to help her stay as well as possible.

> This is my wellness plan. I am giving you a copy because I feel safe with you and I trust you to help me take care of myself. Please read it over now and ask me about anything you are not sure about. Keep it somewhere safe, in case you want to refer back to it later.

> It describes warning behaviours, and asks for help in identifying them should they occur. ("Let me know if you feel I am exhibiting any of these behaviours. I might not want to hear what you are saying, so remind me of this document and that I asked you to help me take care of myself.") It also lists strategies Fran knows help keep her well. ("This is what I need to do to look after myself. Please remind me if it seems like I am not doing them.") If people become concerned for her well-being, there is a list of contacts, including her doctor, psychiatrist, care coordinator, and a mental health crisis helpline.

> I keep a copy of Fran's wellness plan with me at all times, but it is especially useful when she is traveling. It proved vital during her extended vacation in Europe, when we invoked the pre-agreed escalation process and contacted her professional support team. "Having these things in place and committed to beforehand," she

says, "allows me to feel there is a safety net beneath me so things don't get too far out of hand."

Summary

There is nothing inherently noble or positive about illness. Nevertheless, we believe wellness is about more than the elimination of symptoms at any cost, or the endless pursuit of a cure. For Fran, wellness is not a destination, it is a journey. That journey begins with accepting the realities of her situation, and proceeds in whatever direction is most helpful to her. It is a journey best taken one step at a time.

> it's hard work to stay well.. i started changing stuff with the littlest of steps.. baby steps.. the tiniest shifts.. the important thing was that i recognized the little bit i did.. then it grew on its own.. forcing anything was futile.. what's the point if it's too overwhelming? do what you can.. don't do what you can't.. keep everything as simple as possible..

Even with the best of intentions, treatments and support, the road is frequently beset with obstacles and setbacks.

> amazing how i can be doing well for a while and then deteriorate so quickly for no apparent reason other than i have three illnesses that have a mind of their own and independently operate like sine waves.. my life tends to be a sieve, rather than a bucket.. no matter how steadfastly i pour in wellness, it leaks straight through and i am left with my all too familiar illnesses.. but i no longer hate them.. they get to be here too.. it turns out they are great teachers.. the choice i have is to cultivate an attitude of gentleness, courage, and gratitude..

Traveling is easier and safer in congenial company. In Part II we explore how I accompany and support Fran on her journey.

Part II: Do What You Can

I Woke Up

I woke up
Choking
And coughing
Could not breathe
It frightened me

I called
My UK poet friend
He calmed me
He calmed my crisis
Thank god
For the ocean
Of technology
Though it be
Virtual
It be real
To me

And the water
Of word
It means
The world
To me

4. To Connect Is to Care: Strategies for Long-Distance Friends

> My computer is three feet from my bed. When I
> can't make it that far I take my laptop to bed with
> me. If I can't sit up I use my phone. I guess
> connection is important to me.
> —Fran Houston

"How Can You Talk of Being so Close When You Live so Far Apart?"

Fran and I share what is variously described as a distance, online, or virtual relationship. We live on opposite sides of the world, separated by five time zones and the Atlantic Ocean. We rely heavily on technology, of course. Without it, we would never have met in the first place. This is not so remarkable these days. Many people spend significant time online with family and friends. Like us, they communicate using instant messages, social media, voice calls, and video. Assuming access to the technology, the Internet offers convenient and satisfying ways to engage with people, whether they live on the same street or oceans apart.

Some question the validity of our friendship: not because it is conducted online, but because it is conducted exclusively so. The question wouldn't arise if we messaged each other most of the time but were able to meet occasionally for coffee. At the time of writing, we have met in person only once. We are confident we will get together again in the future, although opportunities are likely to be rare. We do not feel this compromises our friendship to any significant extent. Trust and mutual respect are what matter most. These are qualities of the people involved in a relationship, and are neither guaranteed nor precluded by geography. Fran and I are close because we commit to being open and honest with each other, and because we exploit every means of communication available to us.

All this may seem irrelevant if your friend lives close enough for you to meet in person, but there are many kinds of distance, and not all are measured in miles or time zones. It is possible to feel alone in the company of people you have known for years, or to sit beside someone you counted a friend and feel utterly estranged. The good news is that any distance can be bridged. Make the most of every opportunity to connect honestly and often with your friend. Whether online or face-to-face, find what works for you, and do that. This is the secret to closeness—and there is nothing virtual about it.

Three Thousand Miles. Three Hundred Minutes.

According to one online calculator, Fran's home on the north-east coast of the United States lies just over 3,050 miles (4,910 km) from mine in the north-east of England. For most of the year, we are five time zones (300 minutes) apart, so that when it is nine o'clock in the morning for Fran it is two o'clock in the afternoon for me. The time difference reduces to four hours for two weeks in spring, and one week in autumn, because our countries switch between normal time and daylight saving time on different dates. The UK enters daylight saving time (British Summer Time, BST) at one o'clock in the morning on the last Sunday in March, and returns to normal time (Greenwich Mean Time, GMT) at one o'clock in the morning on the last Sunday in October. The US enters daylight saving time (for Fran this is Eastern Daylight Time, EDT) at two o'clock in the morning on the second Sunday in March. She returns to Eastern Standard Time (EST) at two o'clock in the morning on the first Sunday in November.

Fran loves to travel. Since we became friends, her local time has varied from six hours behind mine when she was in Panama, to one hour ahead of mine during a trip to mainland Europe. We have been in the same time zone on three occasions: twice when Fran was crossing the Atlantic, and the day we met in person in Southampton, England. Whether measured in miles or in minutes, distance places certain restrictions on how we conduct our friendship. In other respects, it enhances our relationship or is largely irrelevant.

When Distance Is Inhibiting

The most obvious consequence of us living so far apart is that we cannot meet in person. There are many ways for us to connect online, but we are massively dependent on technology. A power cut or Internet outage can distance us in a moment, and far more effectively than the miles that lie between us. When this happens, we rely on text messages to keep in touch. International telephone tariffs are too expensive for us to make more than the briefest of calls. Intermittent interruptions are no less frustrating. For months, my Internet signal would drop at random intervals during our video calls. I researched potential fixes and bought a new router, but there was little improvement until I had cause to replace my ageing computer. The problem ceased immediately.

Vacations are always challenging. We usually manage to keep in touch, albeit less frequently than usual. One notable exception was when I vacationed on Loch Fyne, in Scotland. I had anticipated poor Internet coverage and took devices that operated on three different mobile phone networks, but there was scarcely any signal at all. Some people relish the opportunity to disconnect from the online realm while away, but I found the experience frustrating and stressful. As we describe in chapter 9, Fran's trip to Europe in the summer of 2013 was an immense challenge. Access to the Internet was patchy and far more expensive for Fran than when she is at home. We mostly relied on instant messaging to keep in touch. Voice calls were possible, but infrequent. We managed one short video call in more than three months.

Even when the technology works, there are times when nothing can compensate for the lack of physical presence. I cannot offer Fran the kind of practical help I would if we lived closer. I cannot accompany her to appointments, drive her to the launderette, shovel snow from her driveway, or help with repairs around the house. Physical expressions of support and comfort are also denied us, such as the pressure of a hand held, or the hug that says, "I am here." There have been occasions when the miles between us have been hard to dismiss.

In October 2012, Hurricane Sandy bore down on the East Coast of America. Fran lived alone and was naturally anxious as the region prepared for the hurricane's arrival. It caused no significant damage where Fran lived, but for several days afterwards, she was unable to contact family in the more affected inland areas. I helped her track down information and emergency numbers but as I wrote in my diary, "I feel so very far from Fran right now." The following February, Fran hunkered down to await the arrival of what had been dubbed Winter Storm Nemo. Of greatest concern to us was the risk to Fran's electrical supply and telecommunications. There had been a power outage across the region only days before. A prolonged blackout would leave her without light, heating, refrigeration, and Internet access; it might mean abandoning her home altogether to stay in one of the local emergency centres. She was as prepared as she could be, but anxious to be facing it alone. The storm passed without significant disruption, but brought record-breaking snowfall to the area.

On occasion, my sense of helplessness has been compounded by technical difficulties. The following account is from October 2012. I was on vacation in the English Lake District at the time.

I'd been looking forward to meeting Fran on webcam tonight but the call kept dropping. We switched to voice but even that wouldn't work. Chat was OK, but it took a while for me to get past my frustrations. Fran was very calm and sensible, but it wasn't really what I wanted to hear. I was pretty grouchy! Then she said there'd just been an earthquake! I couldn't believe it! I chatted with her until well after one o'clock in the morning. I felt helpless and didn't know what to do or say that could possibly help. Fran was shaken and worried about people who might be affected. Then she dismissed me so I could go to bed. She didn't have the energy to handle my distress as well as hers.

The magnitude 4.6 earthquake struck the state of Maine at 7:12 p.m. local time (twelve minutes past midnight in the UK). The epicentre lay twenty miles (thirty-two kilometers) to the west of Portland. It hurt that Fran didn't want me to stay on with her, but I could be of little practical help and she needed to handle things in her own way.

When Distance Is Enhancing

It might seem as though a five hour time difference would make it difficult for us to connect, but our lives mesh well. On a typical day we talk briefly in the morning and meet twice later for video calls, usually at two o'clock in the afternoon and six o'clock in the evening for Fran (seven and eleven o'clock in the evening for me). This regular scheduling provides stability and structure, which are otherwise lacking in a life governed by illness. In our experience, a live video call is every bit as real as a face-to-face conversation. Meeting on webcam in our homes allows us to focus on what we are saying to each other with little in the way of external distractions. The experience is further enhanced by us having access to online services such as search engines, social media, music, video, and shared documents during a call. These are generally unavailable when friends meet socially face-to-face.

Our Internet friendship has one further advantage: an historical record that means we can revisit many of our conversations months, or even years, after they took place. E-mail is the most obvious record, but social networking sites also retain posts, comments, and instant messages. These archives have been invaluable in writing this book, enabling us to include examples of our conversation throughout the course of our friendship. We use them in a similar way ourselves when we want to recall approaches and situations we found beneficial—or troublesome—in the past. They supplement other notes and journals, such as my personal diary and the collection of notebooks Fran filled during one prolonged episode of mania. The ability to revisit conversations and shared experiences adds value to a relationship. One friend expressed it to me in this way:

"Thank you for sharing all of these thoughts with me, Marty. I like that I have them to keep. I consider them boosters: little joys that help me to feel more upbeat."

Learning to handle physical separation in my friendship with Fran has benefited my life generally. The most dangerous and insidious separations are internal. Emotional withdrawal, embarrassment, insecurity, anxiety, depression, and the fear—real or imagined—of rejection can all isolate people, no matter the nature of their relationships or how close they live to one another. Fran and I have had to find ways to mitigate the impact of living so far apart. We have learned to accept the limitations of our situation and focus on the possible. We exploit the many channels of communication open to us. Communication builds trust, respect, and resilience. If one channel fails (whether for technical or personal reasons) there is usually another we can turn to. We work hard to restore broken connections and continue where we left off. These skills and approaches translate directly to other situations and other relationships.

When Distance Is Irrelevant

When I am on a voice or video call, exchanging instant messages, or interacting on a social networking site, it makes little difference where in the world the other person is physically located. I can message Fran on the other side of the world as easily as I message my son upstairs in his bedroom. I edit her letters and e-mail messages—and we have co-written this book—as readily as if we lived in the same town, or were sitting together in the same room. It would be easier to investigate issues with Fran's computer or mobile phone if I could call round in person, but with the right technology, some imagination, and plenty of patience there is little we cannot work around. Of course, most of the time we are not editing documents, diagnosing technical glitches, or writing books together. We are doing what friends do the world over, whether they meet online or in their local coffee shop. We hang out. We talk. We listen and support each other. We share our thoughts, problems, and ideas. We care.

It's Good to Talk. And Chat. And Text. And Cam.

There are many ways to connect and each has its unique virtues, limitations, and character. If I want to check what time we are to meet in the evening, I send Fran a social media message. If she asks me to remind her to get up early and put out the trash, I choose SMS, because the text alert on her phone is louder and more likely to wake her than the beep of an incoming chat message. If I want to share what is going on around me right now, I take a photograph on my phone and send it in an e-mail or instant message. Voice and video calls bring us immediately into each other's presence. Sometimes, only a handwritten letter will suffice.

The Written Word

We love writing and word-play. From our very first meeting online, the written word has been the foundation of our friendship. We continue to write to each other freely and frequently.

Instant Messages (Chat)

The immediacy of instant messaging (social media chat) makes it our number one way to keep in touch. We use it for everything from a quick hello or question, to lengthy discussions about whatever is happening for us at the time. Most of the conversations in this book are drawn from our archive of instant messages.

Text Messages (SMS)

International text messages (otherwise known as Short Message Service messages, or SMS) are relatively expensive to send, but they are useful if we cannot communicate online for any reason. This was the case when Fran was sailing between the US and Europe. I sent a short text message to Fran each morning and evening so she knew I was thinking of her and did not feel isolated from the outside world.

E-mail

Fran and I used e-mail a great deal when we were first friends, and I soon found myself copied into her e-mail exchanges with others. When she is manic, she has a tendency to bombard her closest friends with messages. She copies several of us at a time into individual e-mails, and forwards messages she receives from other people to everyone in the group. This strategy helps Fran process her streaming thoughts and solicit input from those she most trusts, but it can be overwhelming for the rest of us. Instant messaging has largely replaced e-mail for our day-to-day conversations. We mainly use e-mail to communicate with other people, or to exchange images and documents.

Handwritten Letters

It can take up to a week for a letter posted in the UK to be delivered to the US. It might seem pointless to send a letter when the message could be transmitted electronically in an instant, but speed is not always the prime consideration. In a friendship conducted almost exclusively online there is something special about sitting at a table in my favourite coffee shop, taking up my fountain pen and writing a letter, then sealing the letter into an envelope, addressing it, and taking it to the post office. The fact that a week may elapse before my words reach Fran enhances their significance rather than diminishing it. In a letter, I pay less attention to our day-to-day situation, problems, and activities, and explore more general themes operating on longer timescales. Fran often reads my letters to me once they have reached her.

Internet File Sharing

We use Internet (cloud-based) file storage and sharing services as an alternative to e-mailing files back and forth between us. This is especially useful when we need to work on documents together, or even at the same time. Fran's sleep diary, wellness plan, and our various to-do lists are all good examples. This book is the best example of all. It was written and edited collaboratively using a cloud-based editing suite, with all the documents stored online in shared folders.

Sight and Sound

If the written word forms the foundation of our friendship, voice and video calls add richness and depth.

Voice Calls

We had been friends for about a month, communicating using e-mail and chat messages, when Fran suggested trying an Internet telephony service (also called Voice over IP, or VOIP) so we could talk together. I hesitated at first. I had never been confident on the telephone, and the prospect of speaking to my new friend on the other side of the world was daunting, despite us having shared a great deal already. I took a few days to think about it, then registered an account. Our first conversation took place on a Saturday in June, as I recorded in my diary that evening.

> I went to the Green Festival in Leazes Park. True to my word, I messaged Fran to ask if she still wanted to talk. After all my nervousness, I wasn't scared at all, and we got on perfectly. We must have been talking for at least an hour. I don't know how often we will talk like that, but we now know that we can.

Our first call was a perfect introduction to the delights—and frustrations—of Internet telephony. It was delightful to hear Fran's accent and for her to hear mine. ("I love your voice, Fran!" "I love yours!") I explored the festival site as we talked so Fran could hear the sounds and music going on around me. We also learned that Internet calls require a stable data signal at each end, and that restoring a dropped connection is not always as straightforward as one might think.

Until we started using video, we spoke on the telephone up to three or four hours a day. We still have a brief call each morning (around seven o'clock for Fran, noon for me) to confirm our plans for the coming day. By using Internet telephony applications (apps) on our cell phones we can share whatever we are doing wherever we are, whether that is sitting in a café or restaurant, walking on the beach or to an appointment, or shopping for groceries. Taking each other "out and about" like this broadens our understanding of each other's lives immensely. Most of our video calls are made indoors when we are sitting at our computers.

Video Calls

We had been friends for six months before we tried a video call, but it was a resounding success. We now "cam" twice a day when our schedules and other priorities allow. Spending so much time face-to-face has given us a deep, and mostly subconscious, awareness of the other's natural demeanour. Fran often deduces my mood without me needing to state it, and I am able to spot subtle changes in Fran's behaviour or appearance that might suggest an unhealthy drift towards mania or depression. There is nothing uncanny about this; it is what happens when people know each other well. It reinforces our assertion that a meaningful understanding of another person is possible without necessarily meeting in the same physical space.

During our first December as friends, Fran was in a deep depression after spending most of the previous year in mania. She felt bereft, isolated, suicidal, and alone. It meant a great deal to her that she could spend time on webcam with me and my family over Christmas and New Year. We opened our presents together, and Fran kept me company in the kitchen on Christmas morning as I cooked dinner, my netbook perched precariously on top of the saucepan stand. Fran told me later it was the best Christmas she had ever spent.

Sharing Our World and Our Lives

We have seen how we use the written word, voice calls, and video to keep in touch, but growing our successful, mutually supportive friendship involves more than the exchange of words. It involves us sharing the richness of our lives, our worlds, our interests, and cultures.

Sharing Our Senses

Sounds
The most important sounds we can ever share with another person are our own voices. Fran and I enjoy reading to each other: our favourite poetry, articles we have encountered online, or anything else that catches our imagination. I once helped Fran select passages from her first book to read at a local book-signing event, and sat with her over a number of evenings as she rehearsed her presentation and timings. Fran has difficulty maintaining her focus for long, and finds lengthy works easier to digest if they are read to her. We have enjoyed a wide range of fiction and non-fiction books in this way, including a series of thrillers by a friend of Fran's.

> There is nothing better than a well-written thriller.. and nothing better than it being set in your hometown.. and actually knowing the author.. but when you have an Englishman reading it to you.. that takes the cake..

If Fran's health prevents her from attending a local concert, we search for the artist's music online, and hold a private concert at home. Internet television, radio, and movie channels offer further opportunities to share quality time together. We have become familiar with the sounds of each other's neighbourhoods: foghorns, police sirens, traffic, street musicians, and birdsong. But silence is also a sound, and sometimes we are quiet together, sharing the moment without needing to fill the space with talking.

Sights
The most mundane of details can appear exotic when seen through new eyes. As keen amateur photographers we share what we encounter as we go about our daily business: cattle in a park on my way to work, the view from my office, the interior of my favourite coffee bar, Fran's favourite restaurant or theatre, the view from a ferry boat or train, our homes, friends, and families. Sharing in this way deepens our knowledge of each

other's environments, and makes us more appreciative of our own. Video adds a further dimension, whether the subject is an art installation, a friend's book reading, a birthday party, or a street performance of *Hamlet*.

Taste and Smell

As a first Christmas present, Fran sent me a generous sample of her beloved hazelnut coffee: I thanked her with a selection of locally roasted coffees from my home city of Newcastle. We have exchanged tea bags, cookies, candies and chocolate, and Fran's homemade banana bread has become an annual Christmas treat for me and my family.

Sharing Our Worlds

Location-based social networking services allow people to share their geographical locations with others. The person who receives the invitation can track their friend in real time on a detailed map or satellite image. Fran and I use one such service as the virtual equivalent of taking a walk together. I have accompanied her as she walks on the beach, cycles around her neighbourhood, or travels to and from appointments. In turn, she can follow me as I explore my city, take walks in the countryside, or travel home from work. Web-based mapping services allow virtual journeys around many of the world's towns and cities. The views are not up to date, but the panoramic images are highly detailed and the experience is dynamic and immersive.

These technologies can be used together, as I did when Fran visited the town of Sitges, near Barcelona in Spain. She shared her location with me, and invited me to follow as she explored the old town and seafront. While we chatted using instant messaging, I took the equivalent walk on my computer. We stopped at a restaurant. In virtual terms, I had to remain outside, but the photograph Fran e-mailed me of the view from her table by the window matched almost perfectly what I could see on my computer screen. These services have been extended to include some building interiors. I recently accompanied Fran to a charity fundraiser held in a waterside restaurant. I explored the place virtually on my computer while Fran ordered her meal and sent me photographs from her cell phone. We shared a short video call, during which Fran introduced me to a slightly bemused waitress. "It's my best friend Marty, from England!"

Sharing Our Interests and Culture

Fran and I have many interests in common, but also enjoy exploring our differences. We see these as opportunities to learn more about each other and our respective cultures.

Family and Friends

Although we connect almost every day, our get-togethers often need to be fitted around other people, responsibilities and appointments. Now and again, we set time aside and make a specific commitment to get together, just as we would if we were arranging to meet for coffee or attend an appointment together. This helps remind us—and others—that a distance friendship such as ours is no less real or important than any other. Technology doesn't only allow us to connect with each other. I have spoken to many of Fran's friends, some of her professional support team, and several members of her family. She has likewise met friends of mine, my wife, children, mother, and sister. Connecting like this affirms the validity of our friendship in the eyes of other significant people in our lives, who may have little previous experience of online, distance relationships.

The Arts

The city of Portland, Maine, has a vibrant art community. Fran goes to the theatre and cinema, and attends concerts, gallery openings, and exhibitions whenever her health permits. I cannot accompany her in person, but she takes photos and videos to share with me, and we make a point of discussing her experiences afterwards. I do the same with events I attend here in the UK.

Sport

Fran is passionate about hockey, baseball, and the National Football League—especially the annual Super Bowl championship game. I have little personal interest in sport, but I enjoy watching key events with Fran. My wife shares Fran's abiding love of horses and horse racing. The three of us have watched several Triple Crown races together, my wife and I following Fran's live television coverage of the action on webcam.

Travel

Travel can be hard for people living with mental illness, but as Fran herself puts it, "I'm a gypsy. No matter how hard the traveling is I still go, again and again. You are a comfort creature traveling vicariously." It is true that I have never been outside the UK, or flown further than the Isle of Man. I may never understand Fran's wanderlust, but I have come to enjoy keeping her company on her adventures. It might seem ridiculous for me to claim that I travel with Fran, or that she accompanies me on holidays in the UK. Yet we stay closely in touch, and share our experiences as fully as possible. My horizons have certainly been broadened as Fran's virtual travel companion on trips to The Bahamas, Panama, Spain, and on a three-month tour of central Europe. As we describe in chapter 9, I have witnessed both the negative and the positive impact of travel on Fran's health and well-being, as she challenges herself to explore new environments, meet new people, and discover more about herself.

Summary

Having read this chapter, you may be wondering what business it has in a book about being a supportive friend to someone who lives with mental illness. We have talked about how technology can be used to build and maintain a relationship with someone on the other side of the world. What does this have to say to you and your friend, if you live close to each other and can meet in person any time you wish? Fran's illnesses affect her life and our friendship in many ways, and most of this book focuses on how we handle those realities. But Fran is much more than the sum of her illnesses and the same is undoubtedly true of your friend.

Like yours, our relationship is complex and complicated: at times tear-filled, frequently uncertain, and occasionally joyful. All relationships have issues. All friends know something about the distances that can develop between two people, and—if the friendship has any mileage at all—about bridging those distances. In this chapter, we have shown how Fran and I bridge the three thousand miles and five time zones which separate us. No matter the nature of distance in your friendship, keep in touch. Keep talking. Keep the channels open and the communication flowing. Share your time, your thoughts, and your worlds. Do that, and closeness will never be far away.

5. A Hand to Hold: Practical Support, Caring, and Challenge

> Give people what they need. Not what you need to give them.
> —Fran Houston

"How Much Help Is Enough? Can It Ever Be Too Much?"

It is possible to try too hard, from the mistaken belief that the more we do for someone the better we are helping them. This can leave us physically, mentally, and emotionally exhausted. Worse, we can lose sight of the essential purpose of support, which is to help someone help themselves. Doing too much, too often, or inappropriately, risks the other person becoming dependent on us. This is disempowering, and if left unchecked can develop into an unhealthy codependency. No matter how selfless we imagine ourselves to be—and selflessness is neither healthy nor sustainable—being a supportive friend or caregiver can play to our needs as much as to the other person's. It can feel wonderful to be needed, and if our friend's illness is chronic, we have set ourselves up with a supporting role for the long term. Ask yourself the following questions.

- Do you feel proud or protective of your role as a supportive friend?
- Who decides how much help—and what kind of help—your friend needs?
- Do you ever resent other people who want to help?
- Do you ever worry that your friend might need your help less in the future?

Don't be too hard on yourself if you harbour feelings like this from time to time. It does not mean you are a bad person, or unfit to support your friend. It does mean, however, that you need to be vigilant. Sharing is the best antidote to codependency. Begin by speaking honestly with your friend about what is going on for you. Talk about the things you are able to do, but also discuss setting healthy boundaries. There may be others with claims on your time and energy: young children, elderly relatives, other friends, or a partner. You may be ill yourself, or have problems and issues which require your attention. There are also limits to your skills, knowledge, and competence. No one can tell you where the boundaries ought to lie, and they may shift from time to time. That is something you, your friend, and the others in your life must work out for yourselves. Actively encourage others to play their role in your friend's care, rather than trying to do everything yourself. Keep an eye on your health and well-being too. It can be exhausting to support someone with illness, and you may need your own support team from time to time.

If you devote a lot of time and energy to your friend, others may worry you are being taken advantage of, especially if money is involved. Some may feel displaced in your affections, jealous, or otherwise uncertain as to the nature of your relationship. In our experience, the best response is to be honest and open, although this may not always be appropriate. Most people who learn of my role as Fran's friend and caregiver are interested and supportive. This is appreciated on a personal level, and helps counter the stigma associated with mental illness. Our friendship has taught me to be more aware of others who may be struggling. That doesn't mean I try and help everyone, but I offer what I can and neither absent myself nor run away. To do this, I need people prepared to support me in moments of confusion, frustration, and self-doubt—and they do occur—without imposing limits on my capacity to care.

Play to Your Strengths

I am proud to consider myself part of Team Frannie, the group of people who in different ways encourage, help, and support her.

Health and social care practitioners, friends, and family members offer whatever we are best equipped to provide. You likewise have a unique role to play in your friend's support team. The makeup of the team is likely to change over time. Professionals move on, or your friend may decide to look for a new doctor, psychiatrist, or therapist. Friends also come and go. Many who knew Fran when she was stable or in depression backed away from her during a lengthy episode of mania. Some of these relationships resumed afterwards, but not all. Fran has compassion for those who were unable to handle her at that time: "I was too much, too close." Nevertheless, the hurt remains.

Being part of a team means playing to your strengths, accepting there are limits to what you can do, and allowing fellow team members to do the same. Local friends support Fran in ways I cannot, but there is much I can do. I provide technical assistance when her gadgets are not working properly, proofread and edit correspondence, help plan trips away, and research online. Like anyone, well or ill, Fran also needs companionship, understanding, and moral support. The five hour time difference means I am often more available to her than friends who live locally. It is fortunate that I have time and energy to share with Fran, and a partner amenable to me doing so. Equally fortunate is our shared belief that online, distance relationships can be genuinely and deeply meaningful.

Fran once called me from the airport as she was about to take an extended trip abroad. A friend had told her she had "real guts" to be making the journey. It was a simple enough thing for someone to say, but it meant a great deal to her. Another friend gave her a different gift: "Have a great time. See you when you get back." His down-to-earth attitude helped her see the trip for the simple adventure it was, and granted her the freedom to experience it without feeling tied to people back home. As we talked, I wondered what I was offering in relation to the journey. We were unlikely to be in touch anywhere near as much as usual, and I had told her many times how much I would miss her. My doubts betrayed a lack of trust and must surely be a burden to her, rather than the support and encouragement she needed. But I realised my honesty was a gift in itself. By acknowledging how I was feeling at the start of the trip, I could then let it go and focus on Fran's needs. She knew I supported her going away. I had spent every day of the previous four weeks helping her prepare. More than anyone else, I would provide a sense of continuity for us both while she was away. Mine would be the shoulder she leaned on—and cried on—in the coming months. To use Fran's phrase, I would be the one holding the string of her balloon. We explore what happened during that trip in chapter 9.

I asked Fran to tell me the three most important ways I help her. Without hesitation, she replied: "Being there always, technical support, writing and editing." I have added two more: advocacy and challenge.

Being There Always

Fran and I are respectful of each other's privacy, relationships, and need for personal space, but it is rare for us to go twenty-four hours without being in touch. That might suggest an unhealthy degree of codependency, but a distinction can be drawn between overreliance and commitment. It would be unsustainable for me to make myself available to Fran at a moment's notice, disregarding my needs and those of other people in my life. It is, nonetheless, a cornerstone of our friendship that Fran can contact me without worrying about time differences or if I am likely to be available. She knows I will never ignore her and will always respond, even if it is to say I am busy and will get back to her when I can. This commitment is important to us both. We had been friends a few months when I told Fran, "You're stuck with me now. I hope you realise that." Her reply captured the essence of our friendship perfectly: "Like gum on my shoe."

Being there for Fran includes helping her stay on track, vigilance, planning and research, being present in times of need, and companionship.

Staying on Track

We involve each other closely in our plans and activities, and use an online calendar to keep track of appointments and meetings. Fran has a good memory but tends to lose focus when she is depressed, severely fatigued, or in pain. In mania, she can be intensely focused on what she is doing, but other things are likely to be overlooked. She sometimes asks me to remind her about specific tasks, such as putting out the trash, paying monthly bills on time, taking a shower, or washing the dishes. I encourage her to stay focused until she has accomplished what needs doing. When she is really struggling, I suggest she checks in with me after completing each activity. "Thanks for having me report in for my morning things today, Marty. That helped me. I tell you I want to do something and you hold me accountable." One friend phones Fran every day to ask if she has taken her medication. Some people might find that unnecessary, patronising, or annoying, but Fran values her friend's consideration: "It makes me feel cared for." I take on this role when Fran travels, as I am in closer touch with her than friends back home.

Reframing is the practice of bringing someone's attention to how they speak about what is going on in their lives, and—where this is skewed or negative—encouraging them to rephrase things in more positive terms. It is something I had been doing with Fran naturally since we became friends, without being aware there was a word for it. The following conversation gives an idea of how reframing works. Fran's weight had stalled despite the healthy eating and exercise habits she had established over the previous six months. Her sleeping had also been poor for some time.

Fran: About me not losing weight.. It's just I feel helpless to change anything.. It's just like my illnesses.. And when nothing happens it's like what's the point?.. I might as well stay the same and not do anything..

Martin: Your weight would not "stay the same" if you did nothing, if you mean eating and drinking whatever you want to, not exercising etc. What frustrates you is that the specific changes you want to see (fewer inches, less weight, etc.) are not happening as quickly as you decided they should. I say all this very gently, because I know how hard it is for you.

Fran: It's the same with insomnia, I can't make a difference.. Although I have changed a hell of a lot..

The words she was using ("I feel helpless," "I can't make a difference," "what's the point?") showed Fran was interpreting the situation as a personal failure. Things were not happening the way she wanted, or had anticipated.

Martin: Do you see how those last two sentences contradict each other? They cannot both be true. Change the first sentence. "Right now, I cannot seem to change things so that I sleep right through the night." Then it becomes factually true and less loaded with guilt.

Fran: I can't keep depression from coming my way.. I try to step aside but it follows me.. I feel powerless.. It's the same with weight loss, insomnia and depression.. But I do what I can.. No matter if it makes a difference or not.. My belly was huge when I exercised today because I was being mindful and so was more aware of it..

Martin: Rewrite that last sentence, Fran. Something like, "When I exercised, it seemed to me that my belly was huge." Even the word "huge" is loaded with judgment. Your belly measures whatever it measures today. The number of inches is a fact. It is also a fact that it feels "huge" to you. But they are different. You can change one of them, yes? You can change your perception.

Fran: Yes.. I am slipping on my reframing..

Martin: Put a smile at the end of that sentence, Fran, so I know you are not getting down on yourself for getting down on yourself!

Reframing does not bring immediate results. It does not fix anything as such. However, it helps Fran become aware of deep-rooted thinking patterns which hinder her progress, and begin to change them.

Vigilance

It is part of my role as Fran's friend to remain alert for signs she may be slipping into depression or mania. The following conversation occurred as Fran was traveling home from an extended trip abroad which had left her physically and mentally exhausted.

Fran: I could do a trip where I visit online friends all over the world.. Raise money and awareness for an organization.. And do a book.. And a photo exhibition..

Martin: That sounds interesting. It also sounds slightly grand. Slightly manic, maybe? Just my first impression. Not every big idea is mania, of course. You can do anything, Fran, with vigilance and care.

Fran: I just want to make a difference and do something I love.. This trip proved I could do something like that.. My idea was like what people do for marathons.. They raise sponsor money and donate.. But it could be mania..

Martin: I'm just very aware I didn't spot the dangers with Wild Hair for a long time. But we are more vigilant now. I'm here to help you achieve whatever you want, but in a healthy way.

Wild Hair was Fran's grand project in the year we met. With no prior experience of bipolar disorder, I initially failed to recognise how dangerous mania can be. I actively supported her noble but unrealistic dream to establish a non-profit organisation to help the disenfranchised. I am more aware now of the dangers, and bring any hint of manic behaviour to Fran's attention.

Mental illness can render people more vulnerable to exploitation than they would otherwise be, and it pays to be vigilant on your friend's behalf. On one occasion, I alerted Fran to a potentially fraudulent Who's Who operation, although by the time she asked me to proof-read her entry she had already paid a significant amount of money to be included in the directory. I was immediately suspicious. The piece appeared to have been compiled clumsily from various online sources. A few minutes research convinced me as to the nature of the operation, and I warned Fran not to hand over any more money. She is certain that she would not have been so readily duped, had she not been manic at the time.

Planning and Research

We have mentioned that Fran lacks focus when she is fatigued or in depression, and struggles to think coherently during manic episodes. I have helped her locate and organise material to support funding and benefits applications; research her illnesses, medications, and therapies; and check accounts and bills for discrepancies. She involves me in planning major events and changes, especially any involving significant expenditure or commitment. We have jointly researched mobile phone and Internet service provider deals, and travel arrangements and accommodation for her trips abroad. In part III, we take a more detailed look at how we worked together throughout a three and a half month trip to Europe, and afterwards when she was looking for a new home.

In Tears and Times of Need

I have sat with Fran as she has been in despair or weeping uncontrollably, and she has been there for me when I have needed support. It might seem unlikely that we can help each other, but physical presence is not always necessary. Simply being there with someone in distress, without trying to intervene or make it better, can be a great kindness. The following chapters describe in more detail what it is like for me when Fran is deeply depressed, manic, or feeling suicidal. Such times can seem dark and overwhelming, but I have learned there is no need to fear intense emotions. As I told Fran early in our friendship, "I can't promise I won't get scared sometimes, but I am not afraid." I spent several hours one night talking with her. She was in the middle of a manic episode and intensely suicidal. I e-mailed her the next day.

> You asked me if I enjoyed last night and your "tantrum." First of all, it wasn't a tantrum. You were sharing with me how you felt. But leaving that word aside, I think I said no, not *enjoyed*. I mean, it's not like I was happy you were feeling so low. I wasn't thinking "Hey, Frannie's having a really bad time and says she wants to kill herself, woohoo!"

> But I don't want or expect to only share your good times (there have been many of those and there will be more). I'm not in this friendship to learn from you (although I do, all the time). I'm not in this friendship to fix you (or me). It meant a lot to me that you thanked me for *not* trying to fix you. It's hard not to want to, though, isn't it? When someone we care about is hurting, we instinctively want to make the hurt go away. I cannot deny those feelings. But I know I can't make this go away. You don't need fixing.

> Do I handle you right? Hell, I don't know. In one sense, I don't want to know how to handle you, because that would imply I could manage you, tame you. I don't want that. So yes, I enjoyed last night. No less than I enjoy any other time we are together. Share the highs and the lows with me: the times when you have lots to give, and the times when you have nothing to give. Share it all.

Companionship

It is important to be there for your friend in times of need and crisis, but never underestimate the value of simply spending time in each other's company. We "do the heavy stuff" when necessary, but mostly we hang out the way friends do all over the world. This is especially valuable for Fran, who otherwise lives on her own. We will look at three aspects of companionship: our roles as traveling companions, meditation partners, and weight loss buddies.

Traveling Companions

Technology allows me to accompany Fran on trips within the United States and abroad without physically leaving the UK. Destinations to date have included Panama, The Bahamas, Spain, Germany, Austria, and the Netherlands. Fran often travels alone; having me there in a virtual capacity provides support and stability. The shared experience adds a great deal to our relationship, and I have learned much about world geography and culture.

> As I write my diary tonight, Fran is returning home. I have her flight details and am following her aircraft online in real time. We spoke before she boarded. I know her take-off was delayed, and because of that she is likely to miss her onward flight. I checked alternative connections, and passed the information to the friends who will meet her when she eventually lands.

Meditation Partners

We started meditating together after Fran read about the potential benefits of meditation in cases of depression. We signed up for a free three-week online course, and meditated together on our daily video calls. Afterwards, we compared notes and discussed the topics raised in that day's lesson. It gave us a shared purpose, and the opportunity to explore topics we might otherwise never have encountered. Meditation is by no means always an easy discipline. At times, we have found ourselves confronting aspects of ourselves we were unaware of, or thought closed. As Fran put it, "I think the meditation is bringing up things I need to face. It is making me more aware and I don't like it. I am resisting it." Despite the challenges, we persevered, and have completed several courses together. It is immensely supportive in such situations to have someone who understands what we are experiencing, and the context in which it is being experienced.

Weight Loss Buddies

As we saw in chapter 3, Fran was prescribed lithium in March 2012 to control her suicidal thinking. It was effective but led to her putting on a significant amount of weight. Her weight had been stable for more than six months after an earlier medication-linked increase, but she gained ten pounds within three months of starting lithium. Fran committed herself to shedding those extra pounds and the earlier burden too. I supported her efforts and decided to make some healthy changes of my own. I had attempted to lose weight several years before, but the pounds had returned. We began tracking our weight every day. Fran joined a healthy eating program and began monitoring her food intake. We support each other's efforts and have now amassed a considerable volume of information about how our bodies respond—and sometimes fail to respond—to changes in diet, eating, and exercise. This has been educational in itself. Until starting this journey with Fran, I had never realised how interwoven eating, food, and body image can be for many people.

Technical Support

I have more than twenty years' experience in the information technology services industry. I have been able to help diagnose and resolve problems with Fran's computers and mobile phones on many occasions. I redesigned the website for her first book, and established a new site for our mental health blog. I am also responsible for ensuring we can keep in touch when either of us is away from home. It can be a challenge to find viable and affordable solutions, especially when several countries are involved, as they were when Fran travelled round Europe in the summer of 2013.

Writing and Editing

There are times when Fran needs help to communicate clearly and effectively, especially in official matters. This can be with healthcare professionals, or with organisations regarding accommodation, benefits, transport, and bills. She generally sends me draft copies of letters and e-mails for me to review. Usually no more than light editing is required, but her language can be elaborate and unstructured, especially during periods of mania. This may not be a problem with people she knows, but it is inappropriate in official correspondence. The challenge is to convey Fran's intended message clearly whilst preserving something of her individual voice. It can be a delicate balance. I always remind Fran to read my edited version carefully, paying particular attention to whether the words and phrasing feel authentic to her.

Fran usually provides plenty for me to work with, but on one occasion she passed me the roughest of outlines for an article she proposed sending to a local broadcaster. The idea had merit, but her proposal was sketchy at best. I asked her to clarify what she was trying to say, but she appeared to want me to write the piece for her. I was not prepared to do so.

> Fran, I have some ideas about this piece, but I will not write it for you. You need to set it out. Get rid of distractions. Turn off the Internet. Disengage from your e-mail, from me, from everything for thirty minutes. Feel this story in your heart. Why do you want to write this? What exactly is your message? Dump the words onto the page. Then come back to me and I will help you refine and expand it. I have so much faith and belief in you. I will not get in the way of you being who you are.

It is fair to say Fran was less than happy with my response. She was frustrated at her inability to convey what she wanted to say, and angry both at herself and at me. Nevertheless, she got the message. The exchange was important because it confirmed our respective roles in relation to our writing, editing, and creativity. As I told her at the time, "I am here to hold your hand, Fran, but not the hand that holds your pen."

Advocacy

Fran has occasionally asked me to intercede directly on her behalf. We will look at two examples. In the first, I found myself out of my depth in relation to something vital to Fran's well-being and security. In the second, I felt comfortable presenting my personal concerns to her psychiatrist.

Housing Assistance

A few months after we met Fran feared she might lose her Section 8 housing assistance. The following diary entry reveals how I felt about her asking me to help.

> I don't pretend to understand Section 8 but I think Fran has been refused it, or believes she will be. She's asked me to intercede, to write on her behalf to the housing office. I will do, but I need someone else to see my letter before it is sent out. It is too important to get wrong. She is terrified of losing the house, of what could happen to her if she became homeless. I have no way of telling how likely that might be.

Fran gave me some background information, but the situation appeared incredibly complicated to me. Several people were involved, and Fran felt uncomfortable with most of them at the time. My main concern was not to make things worse by misinterpreting what had gone on before, by reinforcing Fran's misunderstandings, or by making my own errors of judgment. It would have been easy to acquiesce to her request out of pride or loyalty. Instead, I acknowledged how I felt and flagged it to Fran, recommending she found someone better equipped to help.

Fran, I have read carefully through everything you sent today. I do not know most of these people, and I cannot know how they might react to whatever I write on your behalf. You said one of your friends has helped you before with Section 8. What does he advise? I hear your fear. If you ask me to write to them, I will do so, but only after letting you see. You must let others read it too. My concern always is to help you achieve what you want, and not make things more difficult. It is possible that this could, if I get it wrong.

In the end, Fran was awarded her housing assistance without me getting directly involved. It was a valuable lesson in boundaries and responsibility.

A Letter to Fran's Psychiatrist

The second example dates from the same period. Fran had been prescribed risperidone (Risperdal) to control her manic symptoms. This was helpful in the long-run, but the initial side effects were intensely distressing. The following is from my diary.

Fran went to her psychiatrist yesterday and he has increased her medication. In one breath she told me it was what she'd wanted all along, in the next she was railing against having to be drugged up, not for her benefit but so "well people" can tolerate her without getting all upset. I don't know what the increased dosage will mean to her on a practical, day-to-day level. I guess I am going to find out.

After a week, Fran wrote to her psychiatrist describing symptoms of extreme tiredness, forgetfulness, and confusion. In hindsight, her concerns were almost certainly noted, but she felt she was not being listened to. She asked me to write directly to her clinician. I was happy to share my thoughts and observations about how Fran was responding to the medication, although my diary reveals things weren't always running smoothly between us.

Fran asked me to write to her psychiatrist, which I have done. We had a minor spat this afternoon after I asked her to tell me what she wanted me to cover. She said she'd told me already, and I should listen to my heart, to Spirit. That made me mad, but it also gave me the kick I needed. I wrote what Fran later said was a brilliant letter.

I e-mailed my letter to her psychiatrist, and Fran forwarded a copy to other members of her support team. I have contacted her professional team on other occasions, most crucially when we invoked the escalation process in her wellness plan during a tour of Europe in 2013. We describe this in more detail in chapter 9.

Challenge

Challenge arises naturally between us, as it does in any relationship based on honesty. If something does not feel right, we let the other person know, even if they might initially be hurt or distressed to hear it. This degree of emotional maturity is very important. The following examples are drawn from periods when Fran has been in mania. We challenge each other at other times, but manic behaviour is—or can be—the most dangerous and in need of intervention.

Illness Is No Excuse
One night Fran e-mailed me, furious because someone had verbally attacked her for rolling her car through a stop sign.

> i rolled thru the stop sign up the hill.. supposedly going 10 mph.. and frightened a child.. some woman lambasted me.. and said i was always bellyaching poor sick me.. poor "poor" me.. and mooching off everyone..

I was sympathetic, but could not allow her to dismiss the event without taking responsibility for her actions. I called her and we talked for over an hour. I e-mailed her about it the following day.

The way you were treated was aggressive and unfriendly but you conceded you did cross the stop sign, also that there was a child there. You say the child was not in any actual danger, but the woman probably felt angry and scared for the kid's safety. We have all done dumb things when driving, for various reasons: tiredness, stupidity, carelessness. Mental illness itself does not make you a danger on the roads, but neither is it an excuse to drive carelessly. If this woman blasted you for crossing a stop sign then I say she was within her rights to do so, but she was wrong to judge you solely in terms of what she knows—or thinks she knows—of your illness. What I am trying to say is, you having mental illness doesn't mean you shouldn't get pulled up if you do something dumb.

Fran took what I said to heart. She forwarded my e-mail to friends, apologised in person to the woman who had berated her, and spoke to her local police officer about what had happened.

No Smoke without Ire

When we met, Fran was living in a small wooden house. Smoking indoors contravened the terms of her lease, but rules do not always weigh as heavily with her when she is manic as they do otherwise. I never saw her smoking—this was before we began making video calls—but it was sometimes obvious she was having a cigarette while we were talking on the telephone. I disapprove of smoking on health grounds, but it was the threat to her tenancy that led me to be strict with her.

I am not always "nice" to you, Fran. You will not smoke in the house when we talk, and if you do so I will hang up on you. If you smoke inside at other times, you will tell me.

Fran hated me chastising her like this, but she knew I was right. She stopped smoking soon afterwards, although she occasionally resorts to cigarettes when stressed.

Letting the Hurt and Anger Flow

One of the most important lessons I have learned is that it is okay to get things wrong sometimes; for me to become irritated, frustrated, or angry at Fran; or for her to feel that way about me. In a relationship founded on trust and honesty, we feel safe expressing how we feel. If we allow the experience to flow without resisting it, we can emerge on the other side: still friends, cleansed, and perhaps a little wiser. In the early stages of our friendship, I found Fran's manic intensity exciting, but I was shocked at the frustration and anger she stirred up in me. Fran valued the emotional energy and encouraged—sometimes goaded—its expression: "Let your anger flow through you furiously, thoroughly, until it's totally spent. It's beautiful." This was a revelation to me. I had spent my entire adult life trying not to become angry or upset anyone.

We were talking one evening, a few months into our friendship, when I mentioned something apparently innocuous. Within moments, Fran was sobbing and furious. She hung up on me. It was the first time she had done so, other than occasionally as a joke. I had no idea what to do. I called back several times, but she failed to answer. I e-mailed her and said I was here when or if she wanted me. I thought about how I was feeling. I was angry. Not with Fran, but with myself for having said what I did. I had not intended to hurt her, of course, nor could I reasonably have anticipated what my words would trigger. I was also concerned about her, although I trusted her to handle things, however she needed to, and to get back to me when she was ready. As my feelings settled, I was left with a sense of calm. Something very intense had happened, but it was okay. More than that, it was important. I called Fran an hour or so later, and this time she picked up. We talked through what had happened, grateful to each other for the experience. Out of the apparent mess we had learned something new about each other and our friendship.

I have always been happy to help Fran, but the frequency and insistence of her requests can be wearying. Fran understands this, and asks only that people respect her enough not to promise what they have no intention of delivering. ("Yes is OK. No is OK. Not right now is OK.") I am clearer about my boundaries these days, but early in our friendship I felt I was letting Fran down if I could not do what she asked straightaway. We had been friends for about three months when things came to a head. I had helped her throughout the day and evening, but had turned my computer off and was about to go to bed. The description of what happened next comes from my diary, written the following day.

> I was feeling overwhelmed about a lot of things, mostly nothing to do with Fran, but I was OK until she called after I turned the computer off and asked me to edit something to post online about wanting a ride to the Bob Dylan concert. I said I was going to bed and would do it in the morning. Fran said OK, but in a way that sounded like she was disappointed. All of a sudden I was furious at her! I hung up and turned my phone off so she couldn't call me back. I put the computer back on and did the edit she wanted, and then e-mailed it to her. "Here you go, best I can manage. It's twenty past midnight. I will edit the other things you wanted tomorrow. Night."

I had no intention of talking to her again that night, but I turned my phone back on after a while, and saw she had sent me the most ridiculous cartoon video of "Twinkle, Twinkle, Little Star." All my tension and anger dissolved in an instant! Not just the stuff about Fran, but the rest of it too. I called her and we had a huge laugh about it! I learned three lessons that night. First, it is important to respect my needs as much as I respect Fran's. The editing was not urgent; I was tired and needed sleep. Second, I have choices. I might have chosen to do the work gracefully to get it out of the way, or leave it until morning. Having a tantrum about it was also a choice. Third, I learned that extreme emotions can be cleansing. Fran defused my outburst with humour, simultaneously releasing the rest of my pent-up frustrations. As I wrote to Fran later, "I needed to get mad at you. Thank you."

Summary

Being the well one in a relationship such as ours can be physically and emotionally draining; to pretend otherwise would do both parties a disservice. But, whatever our health status, we are all fragile and incomplete in our own ways. Being a supportive friend to someone who lives with mental illness is far from being a one-way street. Our friendship is meaningful because it addresses our mutual needs for companionship, support, and caring. This is an important message. In the next chapter, we take a closer look at how our friendship works during the major phases of bipolar disorder: depression and mania.

6. High Tide, Low Tide: Supporting Your Friend through Mania and Depression

high tide
low tide
edgeness..
what else is there to do but live life..
—Fran Houston

"Which Is Harder to Deal with:
Mania or Depression?"

Whilst both conditions are serious, mania is less familiar to me, more dangerous for Fran, and harder to manage for us both. She can be brilliant and exciting company when manic, but her intensity and self-belief are exhausting to witness and difficult to channel safely. Most problems centre on her interactions with other people. From three thousand miles away, it can be hard to assess what is actually happening and offer an appropriate counter perspective. In contrast, depression causes Fran to draw in on herself. We spend more time together online, so I am more aware of her thoughts, moods, and behaviour than when she is manic and socially active. Her struggles are mostly internal. My role in depression is to gently encourage and motivate her. This comes easier to me than the buffering, channelling, and challenging role needed when she manic. Depression is also less dangerous. We cannot afford to be complacent (as we see in the next chapter, suicidal thinking can occur during mania or depression, and even when she is relatively stable), but we follow the lead of her professional team. They recognise—as initially I did not—that mania poses the greater risk to Fran's health and safety. This is not a general rule, however, and may not be the case with your friend.

All the Waves

The title of this book—High Tide, Low Tide—is an apt one. Fran lived on an island for many years, including the first eighteen months of our friendship. The stretch of water that separated her from the mainland, and the rhythm of the tides and ferry crossings, influenced almost every aspect of her life and our relationship. The title also suggests the Atlantic Ocean, which lies between us. Most significantly, it conveys the periodic nature of Fran's illnesses. In a television interview, she described the interplay of her conditions as follows.

> My chronic fatigue syndrome operates like this . . . [Fran draws an up and down sine wave in the air.] My bipolar depression operates like this . . . [She draws a second wave.] And sometimes they go like this . . . [She draws two synchronised waves.] And sometimes they go like this . . . [Fran draws two waves out of phase, so that one peaks while the other bottoms out.] It's really quite a bizarre experience.

Extending this analogy, imagine a number of differently coloured sine waves. Each wave represents one of the variable factors in Fran's life.

- The major symptoms of her illnesses (mood, fatigue, insomnia, and pain).
- The effectiveness and side effects of her medications.
- Her habits and daily routine (for example exercise, diet, and sleep hygiene).
- Her general physical, mental, and emotional health.
- The status of her relationships (with me and with other people).

Picture these curves in motion. Each has its own distinct rhythm and interacts positively or negatively with the others. This is what Fran lives with on a daily basis. Waves also feature in the model a friend of ours uses to explore her relationship with depression.

> My analogy is a sunny beach. The sea represents my depression. If I'm in the water out of my depth I'm not feeling so good. If I'm knee deep I am getting better. If I'm walking on the beach with waves lapping at my feet it's much better. If I'm on the dunes looking back at the sea view at sunset I am happy and content, at peace for a while.

No one can hold back the tide of illness by willpower alone, but this model acknowledges a degree of personal responsibility. Metaphorically, our friend can influence her experience by swimming for shore or stepping onto dry land. In practical terms, this might involve changing her behaviour, employing therapies, or taking medication. In terms of responsibility, Fran finds it helpful to acknowledge there is an underlying layer of biological illness. It may respond to clinical intervention, including medication, but she is unable to influence it directly. Above this there is another layer which Fran can affect, through meditation and mindfulness, exercise, and making healthy choices about her food, drink, and sleeping regimes. Thinking about illness in this way eases the burden of guilt, and allows her to focus her energy where it can be most effective.

> I may not be able to make my depression better but I know I can make it much worse if I flush myself all the way down the toilet with the horrible thoughts I think swirling round. This realization, that I at least have that power and ability to choose, changed my world.

The following conversation, which happened shortly before Fran left on vacation, shows how we use these models and analogies.

Martin: Are you feeling good about the trip?

Fran: Yeah. It will be fun. I hope my depression lifts so I can be really present.

Martin: Think about our layers of illness model. Being somewhere new and exciting and different is positive. The conscious part of you will respond to that and it will lift your mood. The underlying clinical depression isn't suddenly going to vanish just because you're away, but it's likely to shift in response to your mood. Or think of it in terms of waves. You are "down" in depression at the moment, but you can bring your mood and conscious self "up" so that it helps counter the depressed state.

Fran: Well said. I do that all the time because you can't be depressed around most people, they can't handle it. So it's fake it till you make it, or act as if.

Martin: Does thinking of it as layers and waves help at all?

Fran: Yes. Sometimes it's hard for me to separate things out. It helps to get the reminder.

High Tide: Mania

We saw in chapter 2 that there are bright and dark sides to mania. The first can be described as expansive, creative, brilliant, dynamic, outgoing, and sociable; the darker side as wild, obsessive, incoherent, confused, self-absorbed, paranoid, and uncontrollable. Neither aspect is healthy, nor do they average themselves out benignly. Mania can be devastating, even life-threatening. Its legacy may include drug or alcohol abuse, uncontrolled spending sprees, and inappropriate or risky behaviour. In Fran's case, it manifests as intensity of purpose, convoluted language, feelings of persecution and paranoia, and perilously grand schemes. Most of her problems arise from her interactions with other people. She needs a stable reference point against which to gauge her perceptions, and someone to challenge her behaviour when it threatens her well-being. A safe means of channelling the energy of mania is also helpful.

A Stabilising Influence

I once asked Fran what I contributed most to our friendship. She gave me the image of an oak tree, standing strong and tall. On other occasions, she has likened me to a rock or anchor, a still point of reference amid the uncertain tides of illness. I act as a buffer between her and the world, and balance her thinking, which tends to be mercurial, dogmatic, and strongly polarised.

Confusion and Misunderstanding

Perhaps the cruellest aspect of mania is that it urges a person to pursue connections, yet its very intensity pushes people away. As Fran puts it, "bipolarists destroy relationships." Her language, both written and spoken, becomes far less structured than normal. This can be channelled creatively, but it confuses and alarms people who are unable to follow its twists and turns. The following is taken from an e-mail to one of her friends.

> i am a believer in open ness and honesty and truth.. since i have opened up my world to you.. and you have invited yourself in freely.. i now invite you into my world.. of intimacy.. in to me see.. for education's sake.. for the greater purpose of all the others who struggle so.. i am an open book..

Her friend was sympathetic but replied saying she did not know what to make of the e-mail and found it difficult to interpret and follow. It is for this reason that Fran asks me to preview and edit her e-mails, social media posts, and other important or public messages. Mania is a condition of extremes, with little or no middle ground. People are either on her side or are enemies, and she reacts strongly to anyone she believes is backing away or treating her unkindly. This is compounded by a determination to speak her truth regardless of the consequences. It is clear to me that Fran has been marginalised and poorly treated at times, but not everyone is prepared for—or has the awareness to handle—erratic or disturbed behaviour. Even friends who remained loyal found her difficult at times. One recalls she "attacked her critics, and assailed social service workers who were trying to help her." Another remembers it this way:

At the height of her mania, Fran was at full speed all the time, and her personality quirks became dominant, at times oppressive and occasionally offensive. She sometimes presented awkward moments in public. She seemed to be running on high adrenaline all the time. Her brain worked on overdrive, and her body could not keep up. She seemed happy, but out of control. And then when she snapped, she went down like a rock. She became desperate, unable to remain in control of her emotions. She talked of suicide, and more than once said that if she had a gun, she would use it. Her pain was obvious and uncontrollable.

Responsibility and Apology
In the midst of the chaos there are occasional windows of clarity in which Fran recognises the impact her behaviour has on those around her. The following is taken from an open letter to her local community. It was written as an explanation, an apology, and a cry for help and understanding.

I am grateful beyond anything I could ever say for the help I have received in the past when I was desperately depressed. Right now, I am experiencing the high mania of my bipolar along with the extreme, ever-present pain of fibromyalgia and the exhaustion of chronic fatigue syndrome. I need no less help now, no less understanding, than when I was depressed. . . . Thank you, dear friends, in advance for any help you can give me, and for reading this. I hope for no more than it might open a little understanding. Be well, I love you more than you can ever know.

She has also apologised privately on occasion, as in this e-mail message to a friend.

> I wanted to apologize for my gushing the last few times we've met. Bipolar isn't always easy to manage and I can get overexcited and overstep boundaries. I feel maybe I made you feel uncomfortable. I just wanted to share this with you before I see you next.

As usual with important communications, she had asked me to proofread the message before sending it.

> I don't have any changes to suggest, Fran. It is well written. You know I am never wholly comfortable with you apologising for how you present to people when it is because of illness (if you do something specific wrong, then yes, an apology is in order) but I know you want to do this to clear the air.

Fran trusted me to suggest any corrections. I trusted her to hear my doubts, but I also trusted her motives and intuition. The reply she received back validated her approach. She had connected honestly and openly with her friend, rather than worrying about how her behaviour was being perceived.

Compassionate Communication

On one occasion, Fran had difficulties with someone who repeatedly disputed her experience of illness. Fran drafted a reply, but it was clear she was still hurting and angry.

> Perhaps you haven't explained what you mean very well. And it is my choice to push back what I feel hurts me, and embrace what I feel nourishes me.

She was being honest, but her words were more likely to antagonise her friend than encourage a mutual understanding. I invited Fran to try using an approach based on Nonviolent

Communication (NVC). Sometimes called Compassionate Communication, NVC is a technique developed by American psychologist Marshall Rosenberg to foster compassion and help resolve conflicts in a peaceable way. The technique uses our feelings to suggest which underlying needs are not being met. We have studied NVC for some time and this seemed an ideal opportunity to put it into practice.

Martin: Let's try thinking of it in NVC terms. What need or needs of yours are not being met by your friend? What strategy or strategies can you come up with that will bring you closer to meeting those needs? Start with your feelings. What are you feeling right now when you think about what happened?

Fran: I feel like a child being lectured to.. It's smothering..

Martin: Can you find the NVC Feelings list? Use that to help you.

Fran: I feel frightened.. Exasperated.. Enraged.. Lost.. Discombobulated.. Burnt out.. as in having my light squelched.. Hostile..

Martin: Keep going.

Fran: Cranky.. Insecure.. Leery.. Hurting.. Disheartened.. Discouraged.. Numb..

Martin: OK. Now find the Needs list. Maybe you have a need to be heard that isn't being met?

Fran: Yes

Martin: What else?

Fran: Acceptance.. I've had this many times.. All my life..

Martin: Stick with your needs, not the history.

Fran: A need for.. Safety.. Trust.. Respect.. Equality.. Mutuality..

Martin: Write down as many as you need to. When you've finished, see if you can find two or three key ones. Then work through the feelings the same way. Just the top two or three. That will give you something to work with.

Fran: I can't do this now.. I'm on my phone.. I don't want this to steal yet another day..

Martin: OK, later. You will write a sentence like this: "When I read the message you sent me I feel [your key feelings] because my needs for [your key needs] are unmet. I would like to [make a request, of your friend, or yourself. Something that will move you closer to meeting your needs]." You may decide not to send it. That's fine. But write it in that form.

Fran: OK

Martin: This is deep work. Remember: it's not really about the other person, or what's happened in the past. It's about you. You got this.

Fran later came up with: "When I remember bits of what you said, and reread your messages, I feel squashed, exasperated, and discouraged, because my needs for acceptance, respect, and mutuality are unmet. I would like us to honor and celebrate our differences, rather than struggling like this." She had let go of her hurt and anger, and gained insight into what the disagreement represented for her. It was a start.

Challenging Dangerous Behaviour

Unrealistic and risky projects are a classic symptom of mania. When we met, Fran had recently returned from what she would later describe as a "mania-fuelled exploit." The Lipizzaner Project was to encompass two photographic exhibits and a book. Fran had spoken with gallery owners and raised funds towards the trip, but her e-mails to the Spanish Riding School went unanswered. Undeterred, she travelled to Europe, but when she arrived in Vienna she was refused permission to photograph the horses. She took photographs anyway, but they were of poor quality and the project faltered. She returned home having spent weeks travelling alone, unaware she was now in mania and heedless of danger, trusting to "Spirit" to keep her safe.

I slept on the marble floor of a train station in France after missing my train not once but three times.. I ended up in the wrong city.. I was completely fearless and trusting of strangers.. of anything.. having no filter of what could hurt me..

We mentioned another of Fran's manic projects, Wild Hair, in chapter 2. The idea was noble, to found a charitable organisation offering support to the ill and disenfranchised. Such was Fran's conviction and energy that several months passed before I realised there was little substance to her scheme. Throughout that time, I supported her efforts. I established a website for Wild Hair, and helped draft and edit e-mails to people and organisations Fran wanted to approach. One friend recognised the dangers more clearly than I did. Refusing to be dismissed or ignored, she repeatedly challenged Fran to focus on her own health before attempting to take on the world.

Fran, I am not sure that your very intense approach to educating others about mental illness is healthy for you. I do not mean this to be hurtful, but perhaps sometimes it is important to be direct. Please focus on yourself before focusing on others in need. Only then will you be as effective as you might be in shining a light on the issues about which you care so passionately. From what I have seen, I know you can do it!

Fran rejected the advice, and I was insufficiently aware to counsel her otherwise. Much later, she acknowledged the wisdom in her friend's tough love approach.

Going back to when I wasn't doing well, I eventually took your admonition to heart and started really caring for myself from the bottom up. I genuinely know what that means now, and am thankful for your support at a time when I wasn't hearing anyone very well. Things haven't been easy but I am doing so much better now and I wanted you to know that. You never gave up on me.

My doubts about Wild Hair were finally aroused when I realised Fran was funding the project from her own limited resources. She engaged professional help to draft a business plan, contacted venues for a fundraising event, and talked of a worldwide promotional tour. As we struggled to build a business case, I pushed Fran for information.

You say a year from now there will be a functional website. OK but what will it offer? Are there no other websites already with this information? What is unique about Wild Hair? You mentioned various fundraising ideas and a world tour. This seems huge, given that right now Wild Hair barely exists. How would the world tour work? And what are the funds actually for?

Fran's reply reveals how exhausted and close to despair she had become.

website tabs: home sweet home.. dare to care.. for well ones.. be brave.. for ill ones.. back to basics.. links.. creation.. arts music literature.. links.. in spire wire..

world tour.. i am visiting uk paris rome cairo.. next year.. in each of these countries.. home parties.. with me on the phone.. to the homes.. whoever wants to be involved.. using social media.. getting websites up in those countries.. don't you see.. get busy.. doofus..

funds: i need funds to do the books photo exhibits.. to raise money.. and refund wild hair.. hello.. wake up.. don't you see.. money for equipment.. technical stuff.. all comes out of my pocket.. and i have no money.. hello.. wake up.. you don't get it.. and then i have no time.. to do the accounting and forget that i bought technical and other stuff.. and so it goes.. jeez louise.. no one understands.. my whole life is this.. i get no money for this.. my whole heart.. it takes..

By now, the dangers were obvious to me, and had also begun to dawn on Fran. As she began a course of medication to limit her manic excess, I was able to persuade her to stop work on the business plan and postpone the fundraiser indefinitely. The project was shelved, and there are no plans to resurrect it. It is possible, however, to trace the present book to Wild Hair's original goals. By sharing our experiences, we hope to contribute to the lives of people living with illness, and change how illness is perceived by the well ones in society.

Channelling Manic Energy

Of Fran's first book, in which she interviewed elder members of her island community, one friend has commented:

> *For the Love of Peaks* is an example of something that used your obvious skills to benefit both others and yourself. It brought you into an intimate dialogue with "normal people" (what is "normal"?) which, as you observed to me, was very therapeutic and life-affirming.

I encourage Fran to channel the energy of mania into creative pursuits such as poetry, writing, and photography. During one extended manic episode, we read and discussed poetry together, and I helped select pieces for her to read at local events and radio interviews. I also supported her in approaching literary agents and publishers with a collection of her writings. As in most things, however, there is need for vigilance. Social media provided a platform for her poetry, but also exposed her mania to a wide, and at times unsympathetic, audience. Many were supportive, but others reacted with worry, fear, and occasional hostility. She found this hurtful and hard to understand. From her perspective, she was simply being open and honest about the realities of a life lived with illness.

Over time, and cautiously, Fran has found ways to tell her story more safely.

> The primary thing I use social media for is my writing. I write about the inner workings of bipolar. And I get so much response, because it's actually a real post rather than the usual things people talk about.

She is no less honest in what she says, but I review her social media posts in advance, especially those that cover mental health topics. We discuss when and where to share them, and monitor the reaction to them. As her friend and caregiver, I am available to intervene if she feels overwhelmed. She has occasionally referred people to me if they are concerned about her. Fran's online activity is also helpful as a guide to her mental state. We do not impose specific limits, but sharing more than seven or eight posts a day is a warning flag for mania. Other red flag behaviours include excessive friending and a preoccupation with the number of responses she receives. At the height of mania Fran sent invitations to everyone she could find—especially if they shared her love of horses—and trawled the pages of new contacts for more people to approach. She took it all very seriously, as one friend later observed: "Fran viewed it as a popularity contest, and often judged the quality of her day based on the number of likes and comments she received for her posts." Recognising its addictive potential, Fran takes occasional breaks from posting.

> I recently stepped back from social media. I stepped back from alcohol. I stepped back from coffee. It's not like I'm never going to do them again. I'm just taking a break, and finding other things, because those three things are very addictive.

These breaks last anything from a couple of days to several weeks. Less frequently, we set aside a day on which we have no online activity at all.

Low Tide: Depression

Fran has a complex and ambivalent relationship with depression. She is capable of seeing it as familiar and comforting ("melancholy is useful"), and yet fears its potential to drag her into the darkness. When she is depressed, Fran needs reminding that she hasn't always felt as bad as she does and will not always feel this way. She needs encouragement and gentle motivation, but also to be challenged to take responsibility for her care and well-being. Movement, both physical and creative, is important too. Above all, she needs to know that I am here for her, and that she is not alone. As she puts it: "You help me beat my depression."

Three Ways of Depression

Not all depressions are the same. Recognised categories include major depressive disorder, manic depression (bipolar disorder), dysthymia (a relatively mild, chronic form), situational (where the depression is related to specific situations or events), psychotic (severe depression which includes symptoms of delusion or hallucinations), and endogenous (where the apparent triggers are internal, such as stress and worry). Fran was initially diagnosed with major depression in 1994. Ten years later, this diagnosis was changed to bipolar disorder. Fran's depression presents in three distinct ways: crash depression following mania, winter depression, and reactive depression.

Crash Depression following Mania

There is a tendency for the descent from mania to overshoot into depression, and this happened to Fran in the year we met. My diary shows she was aware of what was coming.

> Fran told me today how scared she is that depression may be approaching. I told her I am scared too. I have no experience of it: she has been manic all the time I have known her. I may be scared, but I am not afraid, and I am not leaving. I wanted her to know that, before it happens.

Shortly afterwards, she wrote to several of her closest friends. As desperate as she was for support, she wanted us to know how difficult it was going to be.

the crash has come.. will you.. be.. in it.. with me.. it will be.. fiercer than.. the mania.. deeper than any dark ness.. i have known.. before.. guaranteed.. and i.. will be able.. to give.. you.. nothing.. in return.. no thing.. but dark ness.. emptiness.. void.. of heart.. care for me.. or not.. your choice.. ever your choice.. free dom.. reigns.. reins.. rains.. for ever more.. end less ly.. this is not.. a light matter.. it is dark.. and deep..

This happened late in the year, and the fall from mania exacerbated her seasonal depression. She was severely depressed throughout the winter. On several occasions, she told me she could not see herself surviving into the spring. It was not a death wish as such; she simply could see no way out. It took a huge effort for her to emerge from the darkness. Her energy was minimal, a situation aggravated by fatigue and insomnia. Fran recalls trying to make herself a sandwich: "Oftentimes I would only get as far as opening a can of tuna and eating it from the can rather than bothering with getting mayonnaise and bread, to save the energy needed to wash the dishes. All energy had to be minutely calculated." She withdrew from almost all outside contact, both with people locally and online. Her creativity also dried up. Suicidal thinking is never far away, but during this period of crash depression Fran was subject to intensely disturbing thoughts, especially at night and in the early hours of the morning. This "stinking thinking" responded well to lithium, but exerted a dreadful drain on her energy while it lasted.

Winter Depression

Fran can be depressed in any season ("I have spent summers in bed with the shades drawn") but she is prone to winter depression regardless of how she has been in the preceding months. There may be a component of Seasonal Affective

Disorder, although she has never been diagnosed with that condition. She finds the holiday period—from Thanksgiving at the end of November, through Christmas and the New Year—especially difficult and lonely.

> I'm totally a holiday hater. People with mental illness struggle through the holidays in such a huge way because we don't have effective skills to navigate relationships or figure out what we need. We think we are supposed to be doing what everybody else is doing. Marty's been very helpful with teaching me about Christmas spirit.

There are signs Fran is developing a new relationship with the holiday season. Hopefully, this will lessen the impact of winter depression in coming years.

> I successfully navigated Thanksgiving and Christmas! I actually enjoyed myself for the first time. The thing that was so amazing is I realised that I actually could change. I was baking like a fiend. I went down to the Christmas tree lighting with a huge bag of oatmeal chocolate chip walnut cookies I'd made and handed them out. I've never done this before. My house got decorated by a friend and me together. I've never had so much joy through the holidays. I feel like that was a real accomplishment.

Reactive Depression

Everyone experiences ups and downs of mood, but events can trigger emotional responses in Fran out of all proportion to what is happening. The news that she would be reassessed for her Meals on Wheels service plunged Fran into a deeply depressed state, just as she was emerging from seasonal depression. She immediately assumed the worst: losing Meals on Wheels would mean a return to unhealthy eating habits, massive weight gain, and ultimately to her death. I shared Fran's concern, but her despair was disproportionate. It was also paralysing. For three days, she found it impossible to motivate herself. Only with my persistent support was she able to accomplish even the most basic of tasks. On the fourth day, Fran was interviewed and learned that the service would not be withdrawn after all. This was a huge relief, but it took many days for her to recover the ground she had lost.

Depression can also be triggered by chance comments, misunderstandings, or disagreements. "Those who understand," she says, "are not swayed by my wavy and stormy nature." Her reaction can nevertheless be confusing for others to deal with. If Fran feels unable or unsafe discussing things with the other person—or where attempts to do so falter—it can take weeks for her to recover. I am rarely asked to intervene, but Fran will share her thoughts with me and invite me to help find a way forward. She values her relationships highly but the emotional upheaval has sometimes damaged friendships irrevocably.

Reminding

Fran sometimes jokes that I am so relentlessly positive she cannot stay depressed for long. That is far from true, of course. Reminding her that things are not necessarily as bad as they appear helps Fran reframe her thinking, but being around "happy happy people" is not a cure for depression. On the contrary, she finds it hard to be around people who are persistently upbeat. My role is not to persuade her out of her depression but to offer a counter perspective. It is important to let her develop her own patterns of healthy thinking. Like so much in our relationship it is a two-way street, with trust as the foundation.

> Frannie, in my role as your reminder-of-things-positive, I sometimes forget or gloss over the darker realities. Your role is to remind me that life is not always as rosy as I tend to see it. We keep each other straight.

In depression, Fran's physical and emotional energy levels are low. She tends to feel stuck, flat, and hopeless. Her instinctive response is to withdraw. Her sleep is fractured and unsatisfying. She talks of wanting to spend long periods in bed. She is capable of watching a television show or movie, or putting on a smile for visitors, but such distractions are short-lived. Often she can only engage for half an hour or so; after that she can no longer absorb what is going on. She needs support, but withdraws from social contact as much as possible. Her limited energy is needed for self-care, and she has little to spend elsewhere. She sees herself as complaining all the time and cannot imagine why anyone would want to spend time with her. ("How can you not be sick of me?") On one occasion, a close friend had to cancel a visit that had been planned for some time. I imagined Fran would be disappointed but she was relieved: "It's best right now. I'm no fun, or I just try to act fun."

I remind her that, in fact, she is rarely stuck for long and is always pushing forward, even when it appears otherwise.

Fran:	The only thing I want more than to sleep or lose weight is to die..
Martin:	It is the depression talking.
Fran:	I can't shake it.. I'm stuck..
Martin:	It feels that way, yes. But you have been here before, and we have moved you through it. We will do so again.

A stressful summer travelling in Europe led to Fran regaining most of the weight she had lost in the previous year. She returned home deeply discouraged and depressed. Weeks later, she still felt a failure, and despaired of ever attaining and maintaining a healthy weight.

Fran:	I haven't been able to get on track since I got home from Germany.. It seems I've gained weight or been stuck.. I can't seem to get back to the good habits I developed before summer, when I was losing weight..

Martin: In fact, you are starting to get back to those habits. You are exercising, eating less, and drinking less. You are changing your routine. You are going to the gym. Your body needs time to pick up on that. It is a HUGE achievement to do this, in winter, in this weather. You get discouraged easily. You want quick wins. I understand, but it's not how this is going to work. Is that a shitty deal? I guess so. But it's how it is.

Another verbal cue of depression is "It doesn't work." The following is from my diary.

I told Fran today, "You know how the phrase 'three little words' usually means 'I love you'? Well, when you are depressed, you keep saying 'It doesn't work.' Those are your three little words." Later she told me she'd been working with that idea and had tried focusing on what is working, instead. The things, small and large, that actually are OK right now. She turned it around. I was so proud of her!

Encouragement

When Fran is depressed, everyday tasks such as taking a shower, washing her hair, brushing her teeth, tidying her home, or doing the laundry can seem beyond her. I cannot help practically, but I am able to encourage her. When the number of tasks appears overwhelming, I invite her to focus on one thing at a time.

Martin: What do we have to do today?
Fran: A bath.. going for a walk.. clipping my nails.. and brushing and flossing.. and paperwork.. and and and and and.. it's all too much..
Martin: So let's take it one step at a time. Put the walk aside for now.
Fran: I know you do everything you can to help me but I'm not doing very well right now and that sucks..
Martin: I hear you.

Fran:	I'm just very very tired of this world and this life..
Martin:	I can't change how it feels to be you. Not directly. I wish I could do that. But I will help you to do a few things today. They won't magically make you feel better, but *not* doing them is part of the down-ness you are feeling. I will be gentle, but we *will* do them. You will brush your teeth and floss, and you will take a bath. Can you commit to letting me help you?
Fran:	And trim my nails..
Martin:	And trim your nails. Thank you.

It is important that Fran commits to letting me help her. In this way she takes ownership of her part of the task. There is no guarantee she will complete the tasks, of course, or even attempt them graciously.

Fran:	It's bath time.. I lit candles..
Martin:	Sounds lovely.
Fran:	I hate it..
Martin:	That's OK. You get to hate it. As long as you do it.

It was as though she knew what having a relaxing bath entailed, but was incapable of gaining any pleasure from doing it. She took her bath nevertheless, and although she did not enjoy herself—"Hated it. But I'm clean."—she had the satisfaction of achieving one of her tasks for the day.

Challenge and Responsibility

When someone we care about is struggling, it is tempting to make their life as easy as possible. This is not in the best interests of either party. There is a subtle difference between taking temporary charge of a situation, and taking control.

Fran:	I wish I had someone to do everything for me so I wouldn't have to worry about anything or think about anything or do anything.. Someone who

would take care of me so I don't have to..

Martin: Anyone who truly cared for you would not do everything for you. That isn't taking care, that is taking control. I am here to do my share, and to help you do yours.

We do not always agree on what is in Fran's best interests, and it is important she feels able to assert herself when necessary. She once messaged me from a bar. It was winter, and in addition to seasonal depression her weight had been rising for several months.

Fran: Having a beer.. I'd like some deviled eggs..

Martin: You make it hard for me to help you when you insist on eating and drinking out.

Fran: This time of year is hard.. And I'm needing something..

Martin: It's not need. It's choice.

Fran: I am buying the experience.. I am treating myself..

Martin: Overeating and drinking when you are trying to lose weight is not treating yourself.

Fran: It's not like I'm out partying on the town with a wild bunch of drunks.. It's civilized..

Martin: Yes I know. I'm not cross. I'm still here. I will never walk out on you.

Fran: Please don't ever walk out on me..

Martin: I never will. How are the eggs?

Fran: Very good.. I must learn how to make them..

Martin: I'm sorry for being hard on you. It's difficult when you are out and say you want to eat or drink something. You don't give many clues as to whether you want me to just acknowledge what you are telling me, or explore it with you, or forbid you. So I have to guess, and sometimes I get it wrong.

Fran: I need to be honest with you, about what I want and what I eat. I don't want to live outside of life.. I need to be in life and have balance, not a rigid lack of enjoyment..

This was not about comfort eating. Sitting quietly in a bar and ordering a light meal was a simple pleasure that helped Fran to feel mature, adult, and normal. I expressed my frustration and concern about not supporting her effectively, which challenged Fran to clarify what she wanted from the experience. Having reached her decision, she asserted her right to do what she wanted. Fran is fond of the phrase "Iron sharpeneth iron." The full biblical verse is "Iron sharpeneth iron; so a man sharpeneth the countenance of his friend" (Proverbs 27:17 King James Bible). The friction of exchanges like this benefits us both.

Moving Forward

Movement is an important part of Fran's recovery strategy for depression. Winter depression begins to lift in the spring when longer days and better weather encourage her outside to walk or cycle, to meet friends, and attend social and sports events. Engagement lifts her mood, even when she feels she has to fake a smile for most of the people she meets. Exercise is also part of her campaign to manage her weight. That said, emerging from the darkness brings her face-to-face with issues she may have been too depressed to confront. She is not alone in this. "The spring has the highest suicide rates," she notes. "I hate spring the most."

Depending on the severity of her depression, it can take considerable encouragement to get Fran to leave the house. I cannot go with her in person, but tracking and mapping applications allow me to accompany her online as she goes for a walk or a cycle ride. There was an interesting connection between exercise and our high tide low tide analogy when Fran lived on Peaks Island. She preferred to walk on the beach, but this was only possible at low tide. Checking the tide tables each morning became part of her daily routine. In Fran's words, "It helped get myself shifted out of depression." Once past her initial resistance, Fran tends to push herself too hard in an attempt to reap the rewards—a lifting of her mood or a drop in weight—as quickly as possible. We need to remain vigilant, because overexertion can trigger severe fatigue lasting days or even weeks. As in all things, balance is the key.

Creative movement is no less important. The wild, personal, and passionate poetry which flowed during Fran's major episode of mania ceased when she fell into depression. Her creative voice was silenced for months. When it returned it was completely transformed. The haiku forms that emerged as she began to climb out from depression were more than descriptions of the island scenery around her. They were Fran's attempt to find a reason to go on living.

boat on the water
slicing the calm
foaming leftovers..

quiet day
loud heart
stillness..

high tide
low tide
edgeness..

what else is there to do but live life..

These poems were written on Centennial Beach, a short walk from where Fran lived at the time. She would return home, show me her latest poems, and then share them on her social media page. It was her way of reaching outward again. As she said later, "I was trying to save my life, to get out of the house onto Centennial and wait for the haikus to come. That was all I had."

Companionship

When her depression is at its darkest, Fran believes she is poor company. She is physically fatigued, emotionally flat, and incapable of taking pleasure from being with other people. Like other close friends, I know my support is both needed and resented by Fran when she is depressed. We are the ones tugging at her, keeping her head above water, when all she wants to do is to sink beneath the waves.

Martin: We will never leave you to face this alone, Fran. That's both the good news and the bad news.
Fran: Yeah.. I feel I want to push you all away..
Martin: Tough. You are stuck with us. It's what friendship is.

It is crucial to keep the channels of communication open. Our calls tend to be shorter, respecting Fran's lack of focus and energy, but as far as possible we meet at our usual times each day. I read to her while she rests, or talk about my day to give her relief from thinking about her situation. When she has more energy and focus we look for opportunities to use our time constructively.

Summary

In this chapter we have seen how the nature of our relationship and the support I am able to provide Fran varies during mania and depression. In mania, I provide a haven. I am someone with whom she can safely share her thoughts, her fears, frustrations, and anger. To a degree, I can also buffer her interactions with others. It is necessary, however, to remain vigilant and not accept her behaviour uncritically. I watch for the warning signs of mania, and encourage Fran to take appropriate protective measures if they arise. Depression folds Fran in on herself. She dwells on the poor choices she has made in her life—real or imagined—and feels unworthy of anything better. My role is not to try and cheer her up but to let her know she is not alone, to gently reframe her perception and thinking, and to encourage her to take steps to help herself. In the next chapter, we look at how I support Fran when she is experiencing suicidal thoughts.

7. The "S" Word: Being There When Your Friend Is Suicidal

The only thing I really want to do is die, really. It is the only thing I have ever truly wanted to do, ever, in my life.
—Fran Houston

"Do You Ever Feel Overwhelmed When Fran Is Suicidal?"

Fran has told me many times I help keep her alive. There is no objective way to know if that is true, but I take her words at face value. I cannot explain my lack of fear when she is suicidal, but trust is fundamental. Three months after we first met, I wrote to a mutual friend.

> I was online with Fran for hours last night. When I called, her first words were that she wanted to die. I know they are not just words; I understand to some degree how real and ever-present a choice it is for her. She should terrify me. I wonder how it can be that she does not. She says it is because I trust her. I guess that is true.

> It is not that I trust Fran never to try to harm herself, or imagine our friendship guarantees her safety. She has never attempted suicide, but she knows what to do, and I take very seriously any hint she is thinking about hurting herself or ending her life. But I trust her to not hide her suicidal feelings from me, and to be honest with me about them. Ultimately, I trust Fran to allow me to help her stay alive.

She Is So Not OK

Suicidal thinking has been part of our friendship since we met. Indeed, it is how we met. One evening in May 2011, I found myself on the social media page of someone who was clearly going through a rough time. She didn't seem to be online, but in the previous hour she had publically shared suicidal thoughts and feelings. There were hundreds of well-meaning comments. People were offering concern and advice, posting with increasing urgency as time passed and she did not respond. I could have clicked away to another page and put her out of my mind, but I chose to stay. We were not friends, but I knew something of her situation. I felt involved, but what could I possibly contribute that would be meaningful to her, if indeed she was there to read it?

Finally I posted something: "Flooding light and love into your world." The words sounded trite and inadequate, but they were the best I could manage. Someone by the name of Fran Houston responded almost immediately: "Sometimes even too much love can be overwhelming." The comment intrigued and unsettled me. I thanked her for her reply. I think we exchanged a few more lines. Shortly afterwards, Fran sent me an online friendship invitation which I accepted without hesitation. We continued our conversation the next day.

Martin: Thanks for posting what you did last night. It brought me up sharp. I am sure you are right.

Fran: i have so been there.. and people mean well.. and it is such bullshit.. someone told her to go down the street to the health food store and get vitamins.. wtf.. she'll be fine.. the bottom line is.. she has to save herself..

Martin: There was a lot of concern being shown, but what I sensed most was fear. I know there was fear in what I was feeling. Fear of being involved in what this woman was going through. Fear of facing someone else's need. There was a panicky selfish worrying, too, in how people continued posting after she had clearly gone offline. The calls for her to come back and reassure them she was OK, that she was still alive. I am happy to see today that she is.

Fran: yeah.. it ends up being a lot of blah blah blah.. nothing about her and what she needs.. all about what others want to give her.. i believe in her.. i do not worry.. that is a negative energy.. it hurts people.. i know i sound harsh.. everyone so wanted to hear that she is ok.. for themselves.. to make them feel ok.. she is so not ok.. i know.. she has a long way to go..

The woman had given Fran her phone number and they were in touch over the following days. Our exchange taught me two things: there is no need to fear talking about suicide and suicidal thinking, and worrying is unhelpful. This is a powerful lesson because we all have the capacity to be supportive—or not. Fran distinguishes suicide interrupters, "those who are able to defuse the suicide bomb," and suicide aggravators. The latter are people who, consciously or unconsciously, impact her so adversely that suicide seems a viable choice.

Suicidal Thinking

Fran has always had a tendency towards dark thoughts ("When I was a child I used to wish I'd never been born"), but explicit thoughts of suicide did not arise until the outbreak of mental illness in adulthood. Specific triggers are hard to identify, but Fran has felt most at risk during periods of loss or bereavement. It is clear to us that not all suicidal thinking is the same. We will look at relentless thinking, suicidal thoughts triggered by situations and stress, hopelessness and despair, suicide by proxy, and suicidal methods. Whatever the nature of her suicidal thinking, Fran is clear about its origin: "My illness is what kills me.. my little flame inside is what keeps me alive."

Relentless Thinking

Fran was acutely manic when we met, and for approximately six
months afterward. She often spoke of wanting to end her life, and
described to a friend the persistent, seductive nature of the
thoughts that plagued her.

> how to make sense of it.. under stand it.. how to not.. have
> suicide thoughts and thinkings.. hmmm.. do you not..
> understand.. the tide.. that pulls.. and seduces me.. to
> leave.. the earth's gravity.. and fly.. a way.. to day.. even..
> and be.. lost in space.. houston we have a problem.. the
> problem of frannie.. and always.. plaguing pestering.. me..

This kind of suicidal ideation—the medical name for what Fran
calls "stinking thinking"—is not constant, but comes and goes in
waves. It is worst in the early hours of the morning, especially
when she is sleeping poorly. Fran once described these thoughts
as a relentless marching army. Each thought must be
acknowledged individually, picked up, and set aside before she
can take on the next. The assault repeats again and again,
sometimes for hours. It is exhausting, and the danger is that
weariness and desperation may lead Fran to harm herself, if only
to stem the onslaught. Her description mirrors that of a friend
who told us: "A voice takes over my system that is stronger than I
am to fight it. It convinces me that I must leave. That leaving is the
only way to end my suffering. It is irrational, but it happens."

This form of thinking appears more a symptom of illness than a
despairing response to what is happening in Fran's life. She was
prescribed lithium carbonate in the spring of 2012, because of its
reputed effectiveness in countering suicidal ideation. The result
was rapid and remarkable. The marching army of thoughts did not
completely disappear, but within a couple of months it had
reduced enough for Fran to handle it without difficulty. Other
forms of suicidal thinking, however, have persisted.

Situational and Stress-Induced Thinking
Prolonged periods of stress, such as Fran experienced traveling in Europe with her parents, leave her vulnerable to unhealthy thinking.

> I really hate this.. If I didn't have you I would have killed myself by now.. For sure.. It's just not worth it.. There are crowds of people who love each other and the universe provides THIS for me.. Aren't I the lucky and blessed one.. I'd rather be dead thank you.. This is not life.. This is hell.. They [Fran's parents] fight over which of us is the weakest.. They say I'm strongest.. Well when I'm dead they won't think so.. I'll prove it..

We remained vigilant throughout the rest of that trip. Fran limited the amount of time she spent with her parents and took every opportunity to do things she wanted to do. As we explore more fully in chapter 10, she returned home exhausted, but was unable to recuperate and settle back into familiar routines. Her home was up for sale and she had to immediately start looking for somewhere to live. Uncertain about her future, she became overwhelmed and afraid.

> i can see everything falling apart, ending up in some shithole.. and that path leads to death.. to suicide..

Fortunately, she recognised the danger. We countered the risk by focusing on the practical steps needed to look for and secure a new place to live. Gradually, Fran moved through her despair and began to look to the future.

Hopelessness and Despair
Fran often talks of feeling a failure, of having nothing in her life worth living for and no prospect of happiness in the future. This may seem a long way from suicidal crisis, but we have learned to take nothing for granted. One reason she feels safe with me is

that I acknowledge her moods without bullying her out of them. In the following conversation I am not trying to make her happy, although humour finds a place in even the most desperate of situations. Instead, I engage her in dialogue and help shift her towards choosing something positive to do for herself.

Fran: I don't like stepping out of my home. It seems everyone is doing so well. Moving on. Expanding. And I feel stuck. Everyone my age has homes and relationships and is financially secure.

Martin: Let's balance that a little. Yes you are surrounded by successful people, but you know there are many who are destitute or homeless.

Fran: I know, but it doesn't resonate in my heart. I'm obviously not happy. Far from it. I'm depressed and nothing I can do will shift it. I do all these nice little habits until I get an upswing, and then I have to worry about it going too far and getting manic. This sucks.

Martin: My hand in yours.

Fran: I don't even want your hand. I push you away. I guess it's the depression talking. I just wanna be left alone to die.

Martin: I will never do that. Hate me for that if you want to. Did you talk with your friend?

Fran: Yes but I acted as if I was ok.

Martin: I'm glad you don't need to do that with me.

Fran: Lucky you. He knows without me telling him.

Martin: Yes I am lucky. But I am not better than you. We are equals.

Fran: Hogwash.

Martin: You have illness. You are depressed, but not bad, or less than. Do they really wash hogs?

Fran: I'm sick of it. I'm tired of being tired. Sick of being sick. I would like to experience life like all the normal people. hog·wash (hôg wôsh). n. 1. Worthless, false, or ridiculous speech or writing; nonsense. 2. Garbage fed to hogs; swill. Yes. Hogs need to be washed.

Martin: As do you. You need to take a shower today.

Fran: I will walk first. It's low tide. I will stomp on the beach and try to see the sand and water instead of ruminating in my head about how awful my life is.

Martin: Good girl.

Fran: Bad girl.

Martin: No.

Fran: It is bad to feel this way. It sucks.

Martin: It is hurtful and hateful, but not morally bad.

Fran: You've never felt it.

Martin: You are right. I never have. But I listen. And learn a little. Maybe.

Fran: Yes you know a lot about it. That's why you are writing a book.

Martin: Ouch!

Fran: You understand it from a well one's perspective and can share that.

Martin: OK Fran, I will go now.

Fran: Me too.

An hour or so later Fran messaged me. She wasn't happy, but she was no longer mired in her depressed patterns of thinking.

Fran: I showered. Walked longer than I have before. Called a friend. Gonna call Mom now.

Martin: OK. Bye for now. Hi to your Mom.

Suicide by Proxy

I coined this term for when Fran seems to be looking for an easy way out: a means of ending her life without having to take personal responsibility for the deed. She has said many times she would refuse treatment if she were ever diagnosed with a terminal illness, and once became joyously convinced she had a rare form of cancer until her doctor assured her she did not. She has also expressed regret bordering on resentment that a former abusive relationship did not result in her death.

Fran: Many times I wish I had let him kill me.
Martin: I know. It was one of the hardest things I ever had to hear you say, and it was in our early days, too. You hate him for not killing you. Or at least part of you does, sometimes. Just as you hate me sometimes for refusing to let you go.

Many people would be outraged that Fran could be jealous of someone with cancer, or wish to have died at another's hand. I was shocked the first time I heard her talk that way, but she intends neither malice nor disrespect. Such feelings are directed inwards. They are a twisted form of wishful thinking, a longing for something one part of her desires but fears to attempt. Such feelings are far from unique. A friend shared hers on social media.

Back to hoping I'll die of something natural. I know this is disrespectful to friends with life-threatening and terminal conditions. When I had a breast lump in the autumn I prayed for it to be cancer. How fucked up is that?

Far from expressing shock or condemnation, many people responded to our friend with understanding. She was commended for being brave enough to say what many others thought privately. There are signs Fran may be leaving this form of thinking behind her. She usually prefers to be behind the steering wheel, but on one trip she allowed others to do most of the driving. This caught my attention.

Martin: I've wondered if at some level you are courting death by letting someone else drive the car.
Fran: No. It's just easier this way. I love myself now. It's all your fault.
Martin: Good. You don't get to suicide by proxy.

Fran: I don't thirst for death the way I used to. Is it lithium or me?

I told her I believed lithium helped by suppressing the barrage of dangerous thoughts, allowing her to address life on her own terms.

A Means to an End

Fran refers to suicide as "my favourite topic." Most of our conversations on the subject focus on exploring and defusing her suicidal thoughts, but we occasionally touch on how she imagines she would kill herself. In her autobiographical essay "Lessons of the Night," she wrote: "I still do have a stash of pills because I do feel that people should have that right, especially when you are old and everyone else is making decisions for you." We talk about what her stockpile represents, why she keeps it, and whether she anticipates ever disposing of it. I have never told, or even asked, her to do so.

> when i was very ill a friend gave me a lethal amount of pills.. i never asked why.. i was just grateful to add to my stash.. the strength it took to resist that temptation was herculean.. many times i'd take them all out affectionately counting them and googling their effectiveness.. i needed the insurance to escape.. perhaps because this was the only thing in my life i had control over.. and i needed to do it my way, not everyone else's way..

You might disagree with my acceptance of Fran keeping a potentially lethal collection of tablets close to hand, but my reasoning is threefold. First, I would have no way of knowing for sure if Fran had complied with any order or suggestion of mine to dispose of her tablets. Second, an overdose of tablets is statistically less likely to be fatal than other methods she might adopt. Third, and most important of all, I believe it is important to keep the dialogue open between us, and for Fran to take responsibility for her safety. No matter the opinion of others, her stash has been a vital component of Fran's strategy for self-preservation for many years. She voluntarily disposed of approximately half the tablets some time ago. Persuading or forcing her to get rid of the rest before she is ready would not only damage our relationship, it would deny her the opportunity to reach that decision on her own.

Keeping Fran Alive

It is said that the people at greatest risk of taking their lives are those who have previously attempted to do so. It would be dangerously misguided, however, to imagine Fran is safer—or that we need be less vigilant—because she has never tried to kill herself. On the contrary, it emphasizes how important it is to protect her from a first attempt. As she says, "Even if I survived, it's a line I could never uncross. I would always be drawn to trying it again."

Although I would do anything possible to protect Fran, it is not in my gift to keep her alive. Only she can do that. My ability to support her depends on understanding not only the nature of her suicidal thinking, but what best helps her stay alive. Suicide prevention is not something reserved for times of crisis. It requires ongoing vigilance, effort, and courage from Fran and those of us prepared to be there for her.

> What has kept me going and alive is my own hard work day after day, and having loving true friends and supports in place. That is what makes the difference.

Our primary references are her personal care manual and wellness plan, which we described in chapter 3. The healthy behaviours and practices they contain are straightforward enough, but Fran finds it hard to hold herself to them. Despite a dogged determination, perseverance does not come naturally to her, and her volition, cognition, and memory are frequently compromised. Listening to music, meditations, and recordings by inspirational speakers helps her focus. It is part of my role, with other friends and her professional support team, to encourage her efforts and help her stay on track. As Fran puts it, "I rely on the brains of my healthy friends."

Shooting a Wing

No matter how much attention Fran pays to her self-care, there are times when suicidal thinking makes its presence known. When this happens, I hold a space for her to express, explore, and defuse those impulses safely. To do so, I first need to recognise what is happening, and that is not always as straightforward as it sounds.

> Appearances can be deceptive. We have all heard of the person who commits suicide yet his workmates, family, friends all say they had no idea, he always seemed so jolly. It happens. People think they know people, but if they're not really listening, they miss all the signs. I'm not saying I'm suicidal, not by any means. But I realise it's best to save the energy I do have to talk with those who can hear me, read me and instinctively know when to shoot that wing underneath.

Those words were written by a friend who was struggling to cope. Despite being in regular contact, I had failed to realise she was not doing as well as she outwardly appeared. Fortunately, she had other friends more attuned to her situation. It was a salutary lesson. No matter how close you are to someone, do not rely on surface appearances. If you ask your friend how he is doing, do not take "I'm fine" at face value. If you have the slightest suspicion there is more going on beneath the surface, trust your instincts. Ask a better question. Say something. But say what? I posed a question on my social media page: "If a friend or family member wanted to take their life, and you had a chance to say three words to them before they did so, what would you say?"

The answers included the following:

> Think, don't act.
> I miss you.
> I LOVE YOU.
> I would only need two words. Please don't.
> Hold my hand.
> I am here.
> Don't do it.

Whilst far from scientific, the exercise drew interesting distinctions between those whose impulse is to ask something of their loved one (Think, don't act; Please don't; Don't do it), those expressing their own emotions (I miss you; I love you), and those offering a comforting presence (Hold my hand; I am here). There are no right or wrong answers, of course. What is obvious to one person may seem ineffective or inappropriate to someone else. One reader disagreed with the first suggestion: "Distraught people think too much, that's why they've had enough. They can't think anymore. It's too much." The contributor replied: "It's the exact thing that I said to a friend over the phone once. I found out later that he had had a gun poised at the ready and he said those words made all the difference to him." Fran and I independently offered the same three words: "Hold my hand."

How Can I Leave?

No matter what words you choose, it takes more than three of them to support someone talking about wanting to die. So what *do* you say? What is likely to make a difference? According to Fran, "It doesn't have to be anything big or dramatic. It just needs to allow the tiniest of shifts towards life, preserving the freedom of choice. What doesn't help me are people who just want me to change my mind and be positive and deny I have an illness. That is so unhelpful. As is worry." The following entry from my diary describes one of the first times I was with Fran when she was feeling suicidal. We had been friends for about three months.

Frannie called me sometime around 7 a.m. She wasn't in a good place at all. In fact, she was as close to suicidal as I have seen her. [My wife] Pam came down about an hour later. I was still talking with Fran. Afterwards, Pam said she'd been really impressed at how I'd handled Fran, but it didn't feel at all like that's what I was doing. I was talking with my friend. Fran got into bed in the end and I stayed on the phone with her until she was asleep. I called her at lunchtime. By then she'd woken and was, well, not brighter exactly. But she had come back into the positive.

I remember clearly the first time Fran told me our friendship was one of the main things keeping her alive. I was profoundly moved, but had the presence of mind to realise this was not as simple as it appeared. In a moment of insight I said, "You may come to hate me for that, Fran." Her reply was immediate and sincere. "I'm already there." It has become something of a private joke between us, but it is a joke with edges.

Fran: I wish I hadn't met you. I'd be gone already.
Martin: I told you long ago, Fran, that you would come to hate me for that. You'd better get used to it. You have years of hating me ahead of you!

I asked her once if she truly believed she would not be alive if it were not for me. "Yes it is true. You hold me here. You nag and pull and push at me all the time with your love and your care. How can I leave?"

Nagging aside, I help Fran best by staying with her, listening to what she is saying, and then engaging with her calmly. I bring negative or skewed thinking to her attention, offering positive alternatives wherever possible, but I never dismiss or trivialise what she is going through. I do not tell her not to worry, or that everything will be all right. I have never promised to keep our conversations secret if I believed secrecy would endanger her. Fran knows I would do everything in my power to keep her alive, including bringing in other people and agencies if it became necessary. But it would be wrong to imagine I never feel scared or get things wrong. In the summer of 2013, Fran was traveling in Europe with her parents. At the end of a particularly hard day, we shared a thirty minute telephone call, the longest we had managed in several days. The following is from my diary, written later that evening.

> Fran was pretty drunk tonight and I got on her case about that without listening to her side of things. Towards the end of the call she suddenly became very weepy about how much she loves her Mom. I stayed with her until she was cried out, and then we parted so she could walk back to the hotel. I haven't heard from her since. Given how tipsy and tearful she was, I could do with knowing she got back OK. I've texted her and left messages, but no reply yet.

What I failed to record in my diary, because I scarcely dared to, was that before bursting into tears Fran had said, "If I don't make it back to the hotel, I need Mom to know how much I love her." She had never spoken like that before, but I did not challenge her or ask what she meant, perhaps because I had already given her a rough time about her drinking. I said she could count on me to tell her mother if anything ever happened to her. That seemed to reassure her, but after we parted, I started to worry. Had she, even subconsciously, been hinting at something darker? I did not seriously believe she intended to kill herself, but it was a horrible feeling, which deepened as the hours passed. What if she had stepped into traffic, or thrown herself from a bridge? What if that conversation had been our last? What would her mother think of me? Her friends? Everyone would blame me for not keeping her safe.

I went to bed, but kept waking and checking my phone for messages. I finally heard from Fran around five thirty in the morning (six thirty for Fran). She had reached the hotel without incident, but had then been sick and still felt poorly. She had tried to contact me, but the hotel's Internet service was down and she had only a poor phone signal. I mentioned our telephone conversation. She scarcely remembered it, but assured me she had definitely not felt suicidal.

The experience taught me to stay focused on what is happening whenever I am with Fran, and to bring any hint of dark or suicidal thinking into the open, rather than ignore or dismiss it. If your friend lives with suicidal thinking, or has made a suicide attempt in the past, I recommend educating yourself about a subject that can be difficult and painful—yet also extraordinary and courageous—to approach. We look at awareness and education later in this chapter. In an emergency, or if you are in any doubt as to your friend's safety, do not hesitate to contact a doctor, hospital emergency department, or crisis helpline.

A Promise Is a Promise

Long before we met, Fran made a commitment to her psychiatrist that she would not kill herself without contacting him first. In her words, "It was a soul promise, made eye to eye." She still considers it in force. It is arguable how much weight her word would carry in a time of crisis, but I knew from the beginning I would never ask her to make an equivalent commitment to me.

> One thing, Fran . . . and this is something I have wanted to say to you for a while. I will never ask you to give me your word not to kill yourself. That is a lie of course. In desperation I would beg you to promise. On my bleeding knees I would beg you. But if I cannot trust your word already given (and more importantly if you cannot), if you ever reach a place where that is not enough, what difference would a promise to me make?

I once told Fran that if she ever chose to leave, I would not hate her for it. That might seem at best naive, and at worst dangerously close to condoning her suicide, but my promise was instinctive and heart-felt. I also believe it to be protective. Fran later told me how important my words were to her. Paradoxically, they gave her strength to go on. Most people, she said, "try to lay guilt on you about how bad they'd feel if you killed yourself." That argument would never persuade her, but dealing with it drained her of the energy she needed to fight to stay alive. My promise not to hate her finds an echo in the words a friend shared with us concerning her son's attempt to end his life.

> When I got to the hospital that night, I decided that if he died, today or any other day, it would be OK. But I needed to tell him that. So I told him, I cannot comprehend why he is the way he is, but, if he succeeds one day, I just want him to know. It will be OK, because alive or dead, happy or sad, no matter what ... I LOVE YOU.

Other Hands and Other Hearts

I am not the only person Fran has to turn to. In addition to a committed support team she has friends she trusts to help keep her safe. It is hard to overemphasise how important it is for your friend to have a trusted support network. In a moment of crisis, one person may be available to help when others are not. Early in our friendship, Fran was calling or e-mailing me many times a day. On one occasion I was busy at work and failed to respond. Thankfully, she called another friend who made time to talk with her. I contacted him the following day.

> Fran told me you talked with her yesterday, and how important (literally life-savingly important) that was to her. How you know how to handle her like no one else can (I guess we each do in our different ways). I wasn't available for her yesterday when she was trying to call me. I was at work and had to go Do Not Disturb. I didn't know she wanted more than a chat. But it wasn't me she needed, it was you.

I asked Fran what he had said to her. "He said, 'You just need to stay alive until tomorrow, Fran. You can do it.'"

Stigma and Shame, the Other "S" Words

We believe the best way to counter the stigma surrounding suicide and suicidal thinking is to talk about them honestly. I once wrote to Fran: "With you I have learned not to fear the 'S' word. You want people to not run away from talking about suicide; to not lock it away as something too awful to mention." Sharing with friends is one thing; sharing publically is another. Fran is normally very private, but during periods of mania she has spoken about her suicidal thoughts and impulses with an almost evangelical zeal. This has sometimes evoked strong responses from strangers and friends alike.

> Today online, Fran confused and angered a lot of people, who profess love and care for her, but do not see through to the person behind her (manic) words. I am not criticising them, but it's hard to see it happening.

One person was sufficiently worried for her safety to phone the local police, but also ended their online friendship. Another unfriended Fran without even the pretence of support, telling her she should not leave such "sick thoughts" anywhere and should stop "annoying the people around you." Another felt she was giving ill people a bad name, and needed to "shut up and get help." Not everyone was so dismissive. One man, who did not know Fran personally, stayed online with her for some time discussing her support, treatment, and medication. He also messaged me privately after Fran gave him my name as someone who knew her well. Fran was frequently at a loss to understand the vehemence of the response she evoked.

why is everyone.. so so so afraid.. in the guise of concern.. i
am a love.. simple.. and kind.. like most.. mentally ill.. i am
honest.. and.. everyone is so so so alarmed..

She was speaking not just for herself but to show what it is like
for someone battling suicidal thoughts and feelings. We discussed
the dangers many times.

We've talked before, Fran, about how speaking so openly
about your illnesses, especially your suicidal thoughts, can
push people into making judgments about you, worrying
about you and more forcefully negative responses. You've
not wanted to hide the reality of your life from people just
because it is unpalatable. . . . I do not say "tone it down," if
that is part of your strategy for change. But you need to
recognise the effects such honesty can have on other
people.

Fran remains dedicated to sharing her experiences, but has
learned to attend to how much she shares and with whom, and
invites me to screen material she intends making publically
available. The stigma surrounding mental illness is unhelpful and
dangerous to the extent it makes people less likely to seek help,
or speak to someone about what they are going through. Yet
paradoxically, it can be protective to some degree. As Fran sees it,
the taint of suicide would follow her even in death. She would be
remembered not for her successes—her career, her books, her
caring relationships, or the courage she has displayed through
decades of illness—but as a failure. Whether or not she survived,
she would always be "Fran Houston, that woman who tried to kill
herself." As much as she despises it, the shame of suicide helps to
keep her away from the edge.

Taking Care of Myself

Being in a relationship with someone who talks about wanting to die can be stressful and draining, so remember to pay as close attention to your well-being as to your friend's. My self-care needs are threefold. First, I need to believe I can handle myself and Fran safely. The more I learn about her illnesses and situation, the more confident I am in my ability to support her and help keep her safe. Second, I need to know what to look out for, and who to contact should I ever find myself out of my depth. I keep a copy of her wellness plan, which includes contact details for friends and key medical professionals, with me at all times. Third, I need my own support team. It is vital to have someone—a friend, colleague, family member, or perhaps someone in a more formal support or counselling role—you trust and feel able to approach if necessary. I am fortunate to have a close circle of family and friends to call on if I need to unburden myself.

Awareness and Education

Before I met Fran, I knew little about bipolar disorder, chronic fatigue syndrome, fibromyalgia, or suicidal thinking. At first, I imagined I could discover all I needed to know by talking with Fran and spending time with her. I learned a great deal, but after a while I realised I needed additional sources of information. No book, website, or training course can tell me how illness affects Fran personally, but she does not know everything about mental illness and cannot provide a broader, impartial perspective. I seek to educate myself by talking to people with lived experience, by reading books and online material, by taking relevant courses and training, and by participating in the wider mental health community.

It's Good to Talk

When Fran is actively suicidal my focus is on her, not on educating myself. At other times we discuss what happens when such thoughts arise, how she feels, and how best we can keep her safe. Fran is the expert on how her illnesses affect her personally, but I have read more widely about bipolar disorder, suicide, and suicidal thinking. Sharing allows us to learn from each other. If and when crisis comes, we are as prepared as we can be to face it together. Fran is not the only person I talk to, however. It is a sad fact that many people have personal experience of suicide, attempted suicide, and suicidal thinking. One friend told me:

> There is kind of shame involved, in having considered such a thing. But the silence that is born out of that shame leaves others feeling they are the only ones to have such feelings, and that isolation adds to their thinking. . . . In the moment, there is such despair that suicide seems to be the only option. It can feel a logical choice; the only answer. Looking back, for me, is still scary and painful. I find it hard to believe that I could feel so overwhelmed by life and yet I know that such feelings still lie under the surface of my thinking.

I am indebted to her, and to all who have shared their experiences and insights. In the course of writing this book we approached many people for permission to quote from their messages, e-mails, and social media posts. All were happy to do so. As one contributor said, "Absolutely! It's so important. Nothing is more so."

Books and Reading

The appendix contains a selection of books we have found useful. *Night Falls Fast: Understanding Suicide*, by Kay Redfield Jamison, approaches the subject of suicide and suicidal thinking with authority and compassion. The Scottish Association for Mental Health publishes a number of free guides as part of their National Programme for Suicide Prevention. Edited by Sarah Fader, the *Stigma Fighters Anthology* shares personal stories written by people living with a range of conditions.

Courses and Training

The Internet is a rich source of educational and training material. I have completed online courses related to mental health and adult care, including the interactive suicide awareness course run by LivingWorks. Classroom training includes the excellent Mental Health First Aid (MHFA) programme. Originally developed in Australia in 2001, MHFA is available in many countries including Canada, China, Denmark, Finland, Hong Kong, Japan, New Zealand, Portugal, Saudi Arabia, Scotland, South Africa, Sweden, the United Kingdom, and the United States. I have also completed the internationally recognised Applied Suicide Intervention Skills Training (ASIST) workshop. Widely available, ASIST is aimed at caregivers wanting to feel comfortable, confident, and competent in helping prevent the immediate risk of suicide.

The Mental Health Community

Fran and I support a number of mental health organisations and campaigns, including the National Alliance on Mental Illness (NAMI), Mind, Bring Change 2 Mind, and Time to Change. (See the appendix for details of these and other organisations.) We also follow the blogs and social media accounts of groups and individuals working in this arena. As well as providing information and countering stigma and discrimination, the mental health community offers people the opportunity to share their experiences and extend support and encouragement to one another. Some peer support forums are run by official organisations; others are informal or run by individuals. Social media is sometimes criticised on the grounds that a lack of professional governance may jeopardise the safety of vulnerable people through well-meaning but misguided advice. Vigilance is advisable, but in our experience, most support offered in online communities is genuine, caring, and balanced.

It may not be for everyone, but we encourage you and your friend to engage in the wider mental health community to the extent you feel comfortable. It has provided us with information, guidance, and support, and helped us feel part of something larger than our own situation. We have also found many new friends along the way. On a personal level, it has made me more aware of what it means to live with mental illness, and contributed to my ability to support Fran effectively.

Summary

In this chapter I have shared my experience supporting Fran when she feels suicidal. Each person and situation is different, and what works for us may not work so well for you and your friend. This is why it is so important not to fear the subject of suicidal thinking. Talk about it with your friend long before it ever reaches crisis point and you will have a common grounding of trust for when it really matters.

Part III: Embrace the Journey

Urgency

I stopped
Today

Lately
I've lived
Like I am going to die
Any moment
Tomorrow
Next week
Next month

A friend
Helped me

I now know
That
I don't know

I am relaxing
In the unknowing
That
Maybe just maybe
I'll live
Another
50 years
In wrinkles and twinkles and sparkles
To tell stories and secrets
What a relief
For me
And
My friends

I drive
Me

I drive
My friends

Nuts

Thank god
For
Friends

The joy of mania
The joy of friends
I could not
Live without
Them

8. Together and Apart: Handling Challenge, Change, and Codependency

You are my right hand and my left hand.
—Fran Houston

"What Happens When You Can't Be Together All the Time?"

When friends are used to always being there for each other, it is courageous to risk months with no certainty of regular contact. This is especially true when one person lives with mental illness and the relationship is crucial to their stability. That is what happened to us in 2013, when Fran was presented with the chance to spend the summer traveling in Europe with her parents. The prospect was daunting and potentially dangerous, but Fran wanted to go. We saw it also as an opportunity to counter codependency in our relationship, and discover what was left, when almost all of the familiar structures were removed.

There were times when I was genuinely concerned for Fran's well-being and safety, but we emerged stronger for the experience. We learned to let go of the need to be constantly in touch, and to make the most of the opportunities that presented themselves. Months of chaotic uncertainty also required us to relinquish our attachment to specific outcomes. We learned to trust ourselves and each other, to focus on the present moment, and work with what we found there.

A Trip Is Announced

I'm mad as hell.. Mom booked a cruise leaving 6/1 and another coming back 9/13.. Cruise NYC to UK.. Rent a car to Germany.. Harz mountains for 6/9.. Then drive around till Sept for a 2 week cruise back to NYC.. 3 weeks would be one thing.. 3 months is entirely different.. It scares the hell out of me as I would be responsible and have to figure things out.. I'm in pretty good shape right now but this would make me sick.. I don't know if my phone will work on the cruise.. This is not good news.. I do feel an obligation to my mother.. and being with them gives me an opportunity to practice patience and compassion.. But I'm not very good at that.. I wish I could talk to you..

That was the message I found on my phone when I awoke one morning in May 2013. Despite Fran's initial reaction, there was never a moment I believed she would turn down the opportunity. This was a once in a lifetime experience. She also wanted to support and spend time with her parents. But it was not how either of us had imagined spending the summer. Recently returned from Panama, Fran was in the middle of decluttering her house, and had rededicated herself to losing weight. I planned on us continuing to work on our book. This changed everything. If Fran was to take the trip we needed to start planning immediately, and preparations would displace all else until she left. Fran would then be out of the country until September. It was not simply that we would miss each other. My ability to support Fran relied on us being in regular contact. That might not be possible while she was traveling so far from home.

Surrounded by Angels

The first leg of the journey was to be a seven-day transatlantic voyage from New York to Southampton aboard RMS *Queen Mary 2*. We would probably be out of touch throughout the crossing, but it raised the possibility of us meeting face-to-face for the first time. We spent days checking ferry and train timetables, fares, and car rental options looking for a solution which would deliver them where they needed to be in Germany and also allow us time to meet. One evening, I joked that if I lived only thirty miles from Southampton, instead of three hundred and thirty, I would rent a car and drive them to meet their onward connection. In that moment, a hope was born.

Martin: Wait a moment! I could drive down to Southampton on the Friday, meet you off the ship Saturday morning, drive you to Folkestone or Dover or wherever you need to be, and then drive myself home. It's pretty punishing but it could work.

Fran: Even if it doesn't happen, it means so much to me that you suggested it!

It took two days for us to finalise our plans. We would meet in Southampton and I would drive them to London to catch a train to either Aachen or Koln. As we celebrated our ingenuity, Fran's mother phoned. She informed us that Cunard offered a shuttle service to transport passengers into London to catch connecting trains. In that moment, all our careful planning became redundant. I recorded my disappointment in my diary that evening.

I am not needed. Wanted but not needed. I could catch the train down to London, spend an hour or so with them and see them onto their train. But is it worth going all that way for so little time?

A few days later, I was checking details of their cruise on the Cunard website. I realised that after stopping in Southampton, the *Queen Mary 2* would continue to Hamburg. It might be expensive to extend their cruise, but Hamburg was no more than two hours' drive from where they needed to be in Germany. I waited nervously while Fran discussed the suggestion with her mother.

Just talked to mom.. she was stunned.. "what good friends you have" she said.. "you are surrounded by angels".. thank you so much for all this you do, Marty.. you are the best.. she was really blown away.. i had to tell her three times..

Our meeting was on again! Later, Fran and I discussed how the arrangements had fallen into place once we stopped trying to force things. It was our first lesson in letting go of our expectations and allowing things to flow. It would not be our last.

Four Weeks to Prepare

Many people would take a year to plan a trip like this. We had four weeks. As I had anticipated, it took all our energy and time. Day after day, we worked through lists of things to do and pack. We researched travel options, accommodation, insurance, car rental, and the technology we would need to stay in touch. We also gave thought to how we would keep ourselves and our friendship healthy. We had planned other trips, but this was altogether different in scale. Much that we needed to arrange was new to us, and we had little time to learn. I helped with the research and planning, but most of the practical work inevitably fell to Fran. My role was to help her stay as stable as possible, and keep her focused on what needed doing.

> I haven't forgotten my pledge to help you stay on track, Fran. I would like you to message me today as you start and end each task. That way you will see you are making progress. Divide your day up, one hour at a time. Allow short breaks, but when you are working, remove as many distractions as possible. That means turning your computer off if you're not using it, and your phone. We can do this.

Good to Go?

The first thing to establish was whether Fran was free to take an extended vacation. It took numerous telephone calls and e-mails to confirm that her tenancy agreement and benefits allowed her to be out of the country for so long. At one stage Fran almost abandoned the idea, but eventually she got the go-ahead. Her health was the next consideration. Any significant change can be risky for people living with bipolar disorder. Fran had found previous vacations manageable, but she had travelled alone or with a single companion, with the opportunity to rest if and when she needed to. This time she would be travelling with her elderly parents, and there was no clear itinerary beyond their arrival in Germany. I was used to helping Fran take care of herself. On this trip she would also be supporting her parents, and making most of the travel and accommodation arrangements. This was new territory and we were under no illusions.

Fran: I'm scared to death.. If I go I feel I will be doing what's right, not necessarily what's best for me..

Martin: Yeah, I understand that.

Fran: I want to write or talk with you about the pros and cons, to get some clarity.. This will stretch everything I've learned and gained.. And I hope to make progress..

Martin: I think it is healthy that you are looking at it in terms of challenge and progress.

I did not try to persuade Fran to go, or not to go. My role was to remind her of her options, and hold a space in which she could explore things for herself.

Martin: You can still decide not to go.

Fran: i wanna go.. it's just that it won't be easy.. it may stretch me beyond what i am capable of.. i have some peace to make with my mother.. i want an adventure and am scared shitless.. afraid of getting lost.. of not knowing where i am.. of how to do things.. but the adventure lures me.. i want to be there for my mum.. it would mean a lot to her and to me.. it is the right thing to do..

Martin: I think I just helped you clarify some things.

Fran: yes.. thank you for drawing that out.. i will need to keep reminding myself when i feel like giving up.. it won't be easy..

Fran consulted her psychiatrist, doctor, and care coordinator, and also discussed the trip with close friends. The consensus was that she would go on the understanding that she would return home if she became seriously unwell. (In retrospect, I doubt she would have abandoned her parents for anything less than a dire, potentially life-threatening emergency.) Fran arranged supplies of medication sufficient for the trip, and made appointments with her care team for when she returned. We focused our attention on her wellness plan. As we saw in chapter 3, this describes behaviours that could signal a slide into either depression or mania, and actions Fran needs to perform to stay healthy. It also includes a list of people to contact should she become unwell. We updated the document and passed it to her care team for their approval. I kept it close to hand throughout the summer, and Fran took printed copies for her parents to refer to. As we describe in the next chapter, it provided a crucial reference against which we could assess Fran's status throughout the summer.

Tech Stuff

All our plans relied on our being able to keep in touch. Fran enjoys a stable and fast broadband connection at home, but that might not be the case while traveling. I accepted responsibility for finding a solution that was both technically feasible and affordable. Internet tariffs on the *Queen Mary 2* were prohibitively expensive, and we had to accept we would be almost completely out of touch while they were at sea. Things would be easier once they reached mainland Europe, but they would be traveling in Germany, Austria, and the Netherlands, and it was unclear which networks would provide the widest coverage or offer the best value.

Fran booked an international data plan for her phone from her American carrier. This would allow us to message freely, but we would struggle to talk as often—or as long—as we might need to. Video calls would be out of the question. We could extend the tariff if necessary, but that would be expensive. (I monitored Fran's data usage every day while she was away, and was able to warn her when she was approaching her monthly limits.)

Fran would use Wi-Fi whenever possible, but hotel services can be unreliable and costly. As a back-up, she bought a mobile wireless router and had it sent to me so I could test it in advance. I had used one before, and believed it would work on local (European) networks. It would provide a Wi-Fi hotspot to which Fran could connect her phone or her parents' laptop. I tested everything as thoroughly as possible. I also printed instructions for Fran on how to activate the SIM cards and use the device once she reached Germany.

So Much to Do

We divided tasks between us as far as possible, and tracked our progress on shared spreadsheets. The following conversation is typical.

Fran: Tell me what to do next..

Martin: Continue clarifying your to do lists.

Fran: OK.. i will call about my credit cards too..

Martin: We've done well in the past hour or so.

Fran: We're a good team.. You can work on the SIM cards..

Martin: OK.

. . . .

Martin: It seems you will need a separate SIM card in the Netherlands, so I'm thinking get two (one for Germany and one for the Netherlands). They are half price with the offer I found, so it comes to the same as we originally thought it would be for one.

Fran: Yes if you think so..

. . . .

Martin: I ordered the SIM cards.

Fran: The car insurance is tricky.. most places only provide cover for 30 days..

Martin: We've only looked at renting so far. What about leasing?

Fran: This is why i pay you the big bucks..

Martin: Hahaha! My invoice will be waiting for you when you get back.

. . . .

Fran: It seems the more work i do the more i have to do or consider.. hope i'm ready..

Martin: You are not ready. Not yet. But you will be.

Fran: Thank you so much for helping me.. i can't imagine doing this all by myself.. you are my bestest friend..

Martin: Ditto.

Despite having so much to do, Fran insisted on holding the yard sale she had planned months before as part of her house decluttering. I felt this was ill-advised, because it diverted focus, time, and energy from our preparations for the summer. It worked out well in the end, however. During the trip, we learned her lease would not be renewed, and she would have to find somewhere new to live within weeks of returning from Europe. As Fran commented afterward, "it seemed a higher wisdom was in operation."

Frazzled and Fragile

We worked well together, but there were times when stress and tiredness got the better of us.

Fran was really tired when we met today. Not just physically, but mentally drained. We talked a little, but she went off after half an hour or so for a rest. She is frazzled and fragile. She mentioned she is planning to meet up with friends in the final days before she leaves. I said it felt as though our days were slipping away, and she said not to say that because it puts pressure on her to try and make space for me too. Afterwards I wrote a note to myself: "Do not pressure Fran about our time together. Be flexible, graceful, adapting. Fran's needs come first right now."

Under normal circumstances I would have encouraged her to rest when she needed to, but that was a luxury denied us if she was to be ready in time. Instead, I tried to keep her on track.

Martin:	What's next on the list?
Fran:	I'm sorting out clothes..
Martin:	OK. I give you one hour, no distractions. I won't message you until the hour is up. Put your phone on silent. Turn off the computer unless you are actually using it.

One hour later:

Martin:	Just checking in to see how you are getting on.
Fran:	I got distracted.. still doing the clothes.. almost done.. it feels like i don't wanna go.. i am so dragging my feet..
Martin:	I know it's hard but you need to focus.
Fran:	I'm afraid of how it will be when i'm away.. i am too full of worry..
Martin:	I hear you. But try and stay with your list. I give you ten minutes to finish the clothes. If you haven't finished then, move on to the next item. What is next to do today? Empty your backpack?
Fran:	Yeah..

Fifteen minutes later:

Fran:	Clothes are done.. Went to collect the mail.. Now the backpack..
Martin:	Have a hug! When we meet up later, let's do a quick meditation, whatever you want that will energise your spirit. You are doing so well.

Fran: Thanks.. feel like I'm in mud.. moving in slow motion..

Martin: Here's my hand to haul you out of the mud and mire. I am with you. Stay with your backpack task.

One hour later:

Fran: Backpack unpacked.. next i will eat..

Martin: Well done. I will gently push you today. There is a lot to do. But if it's really too much, you get to say so.

Taking Care of Marty

Fran wasn't the only one feeling the pressure. Those four weeks were the most chaotic we had known in two years as friends. I knew I could help Fran stay focused and stable while she was at home, and I never doubted she would be ready to leave on time, but things would be very different in Europe. Far from her usual routine, friends, and professional care team Fran's health—and indeed her life—might depend on my ability to support her effectively. With so much to be done, and so much at stake, there was little opportunity for other things. We set a few evenings aside to meditate, work on our book, or just spend time together, but we were often too tired and preoccupied to relax.

> All our time is taken up with the trip. I don't mind that. Fran has so much to do and I help keep her focused. But it's almost as though she has left already. We will meet in Southampton, of course, but before that is the week when she is on board ship and we don't know if we will be in touch. And then there are the weeks and months in Europe. We don't know how that will be at all.

It fell to me to plan our day in Southampton. I researched likely restaurants, cafés, and activities, but I had little idea what Fran and her parents might want to do, or how much time we would have together. Fran reassured me that whatever I arranged would be fine, but I felt responsible for making sure everything was perfect.

> I count on you to decide, Marty.. I trust you.. You are who I am visiting, not Southampton.. Southampton is just a place.. You are my best friend..

Stressed and Irritable

On top of all this, I had work, friends, and family commitments to balance. I found myself becoming short tempered and irritable. There were physical symptoms too.

> I feel generally out of sorts. For one thing my gut has been playing up. It was the same yesterday. Not painful but uncomfortable. I'm also frustrated over my writing.

It did not take Fran long to notice something was wrong.

Fran: I know you are upset about this trip..

Martin: I'm not upset, but I have some anxiety about the unknown.

Fran: What are you anxious about?

Martin: How we will be, how I will be. I trust we will be OK, but I may need reminding from time to time.

Fran: Yes, you need to trust.. Like me trusting I will eat healthy while I'm away, and trusting myself to manage out there living in the world.. We will be there for each other.. It will be different.. But we have done it before..

Martin: Yes we have. Thanks.

The conversation reminded me I could release my stress by invoking the mantra I had so often used with Fran. "Feel It. Claim It. Love It. Let It Go." The following is from my diary the next day.

I still felt very rough this morning, but thinking through what we talked about I came to understand that it is mostly down to stress. I had just one small coffee today, and I have tried to let go of my attachment to the things that have been bringing me stress: the enormity of Fran's trip, everything that needs to be done to get her ready, our meeting in person, my feeling stuck over the writing. This evening I meditated and then did some planning for the next chapter. It's not much but it is movement.

Within twenty-four hours most of my emotional and physical symptoms had eased.

How Can I Do This?

I was determined to continue writing, both to progress the book itself—the one you are reading—and to provide a focus while Fran was away. We had worked closely on it up to that point, however, and I felt nervous about continuing on my own.

I'm not getting on with this chapter at all at the moment. Sigh. Is it worthwhile? Am I doing a good enough job? I don't know, and Fran has no time, energy, or focus right now to help. And then she will be away all summer. How can I do this without her?

I was reluctant to burden Fran, but I needed my best friend. Eventually, I told her how I was feeling and we talked it over. I messaged her afterwards.

Martin: Thank you for your support and encouragement. It was what I needed to hear. You reassured me, and reminded me how important it is for me to share what it's like to befriend someone with mental illness. It is such a huge project. Sometimes I get lost in the enormity of it. I want it to be the best I can do and be. It helped to share how I was feeling about it.

Fran: The book is enormous.. i forget that.. i just feel you are so competent and up for the task.. to me you can do anything.. i believe in you..

Martin: I know what you mean. Sometimes, when you are coping well and getting on with things, I forget how hard it is for you to do that. Never imagine I need your support any less than you need mine!

Marty's Wellness Plan

I needed to attend to my own well-being if I was to support Fran effectively, so I drew up a wellness plan for myself loosely modelled on hers. I wrote down a list of positive activities and behaviours that were likely to help me through the summer, and gave myself permission to experience fully whatever thoughts and feelings came up, without suppressing or holding on to them. It was important for me to accept certain aspects of our friendship would change, and I wrote a second list of expectations I needed to let go of. These included our usual morning calls, ongoing chats throughout the day, and voice or video calls every evening. I set myself a series of specific goals to encourage me to make the most of the time I usually spent online with Fran.

Meditation

- Meditate for twenty minutes, at least five days a week.
- Complete one twenty-one day online meditation course.

Writing

- Complete chapter 5 of our book and start work on chapter 1.
- Develop our social media presence.

Reading

- Read *The Words to Say It*, by Marie Cardinal.
- Read *A Brilliant Madness*, by Patty Duke.
- Read two other books about bipolar disorder and mental illness.
- Read two books on book marketing or publishing.

Friendships and Connection

- Maintain and develop existing relationships, both local and online.
- Allow other people to support me if I need it.

Self-care

- Take an evening walk at least five times a week.
- Continue to weigh daily and pay attention to my eating and drinking.

My wellness plan helped me remain positive and balanced throughout the summer. It contributed hugely to my well-being and my ability to support and care for Fran while she was away.

Portland to Southampton

After four weeks of frenzied activity, the final days were a blur. The day before Fran departed, I wrote to a mutual friend.

> As Fran prepares to set off on her great adventure, I wanted to touch base with you. This summer is going to be huge. I am trying to approach it as an adventure for me too, but I'd be lying if I pretended it's going to be easy to adjust. I imagine you feel the same. She has come so far, bringing herself to a place where she is ready to undertake such a journey. She's taken each step knowing she can rely on

those who care for her to always be there. She is going to need us no less this summer. I've done all I can in these past weeks to ensure we can all keep in touch while she's away, and I will be keeping an eye on the technology side of things as best I can. Pray to the gods of little gadgets that it all hangs together!

Our final video call passed easily. As I wrote in my diary, "We had a gentle, quiet time together this evening. We were both very aware of the unknown-ness of the summer that lies ahead of us, but managed not to get heavy about it. Her great adventure—our great adventure—has begun!"

Leaving on a Jet Plane

We spoke briefly the next morning, and messaged later when Fran was waiting for her flight to New York.

Martin: I'm so proud of you. You made it. You did it. You made it happen!
Fran: Thanks.. I will be boarding very soon..
Martin: Safe journey!
Fran: I feel so calm peaceful and OK.. Turning off my phone now..

Fran spent two nights at her parents' home. She found it frustrating they were not fully prepared, but took satisfaction from being able to help.

Fran: I told them only critical things for the trip are important now.. Some important things simply won't get done..
Martin: Your attitude bodes well for the weeks and months ahead, Fran. You are helping where you can, but setting limits so you don't overstretch yourself.

I met up with the three of them on webcam the evening before they set sail. We messaged later.

Martin:	It was great to meet them. I feel like I've been adopted!
Fran:	I know..
Martin:	We spoke earlier about acceptance and trust. You have it, and it's a beautiful thing to see. I am calmer too. I'm taking it one day at a time. I've added a table to my wellness plan, so I can keep track how I am doing day-to-day. It has columns for exercise, meditation, reading, writing, and my mood. See how your good habits rub off on me?
Fran:	I'm so proud of you..
Martin:	I'm proud of me too.

Bon Voyage!

Saturday June 1 was the opening day of the Newcastle Green Festival, an annual event in my home town. Two years before it had been the site of my first voice call with Fran. It now marked the start of a weeklong voyage that would end with us meeting face-to-face for the first time. I reached the festival site at midday. The early morning rain had stopped and the sun was shining. It seemed a good omen. I messaged Fran to let her know I had arrived. Her reply made it clear things were not going well. "They have 10 bags. I have 2 bags. The rental car only fits 5 bags. It'll be a nightmare." I assumed she was talking about the cab they had booked to take them to the cruise terminal.

Martin:	I remember an e-mail about the number of bags you could have, and your Mom's wheelchair. They need to phone the company and sort it out.
Fran:	Mom won't change the car.. We are screwed..
Martin:	Stay calm. This will work out. The e-mail suggested a van. Is that not what they are sending?
Fran:	That was only for today's trip to NYC..
Martin:	Oh, you mean the rental when you get to Hamburg? I thought you meant the cab to get you to the ship.
Fran:	It's the Hamburg thing I'm worried about..

Whatever issues there might be once they reached Germany, the immediate priority was for them to be ready to leave on time. I invited Fran to focus on the present moment and release the frustration she was feeling towards her mother.

You had me scared! OK, so something got messed up with the Hamburg rental. There will be a way round it. You and your Mom both need a hug, so sort that out. Then come back to today. To whatever you need to do in the next two hours. I am with you.

Fran thanked me and we parted. The next message I received from her was a photograph taken of the *Queen Mary 2* as they made their way aboard. There was chance for a short goodbye call before they settled in. I messaged Fran immediately afterwards. "Thanks for the photo, and the phone call. BON VOYAGE!"

We Haven't Sunk Yet

I tracked the ship's position each morning on the Cunard website, and captured stills from the bridge webcam. I busied myself with work and writing. My diary shows I handled things well to begin with.

I've had a productive day, although it feels very strange to be so utterly out of touch. I don't feel "cut off from Fran" but I haven't heard back from her at all, and I don't think she has been online to pick up any of the messages I've sent. I've texted her each morning and evening. I've no idea if those get through either, but they should do.

By the fourth day, I was beginning to fret. I missed my friend. I wondered what she was doing and whether she was all right. I told a friend I wished Fran had bought some Internet time on board so we could chat or even have a short voice call. My friend replied, "When someone struggles with self-management as Fran does, it is very loving and accepting to allow that person to manage on their own." Her words helped me process what I was feeling and recognise it as an aspect of codependency. Fran received and appreciated my text messages, but replies were expensive to send from the ship. I did not hear from her until the fifth day.

We're over the midpoint.. It's very hard to sleep.. I've been walking and cycling every day.. Eating more than I should.. It's delicious.. It's a lot of fun.. Hi to everyone.. We haven't sunk yet..

Our First Meeting

It took me seven hours to drive from Newcastle upon Tyne to Southampton, but there were no delays and I had checked into my hotel by the middle of the afternoon. The *Queen Mary 2* was still at sea and would not berth until the following morning. I sent Fran a text message to clarify our arrangements.

Martin: Do we know what's happening tomorrow?
Fran: Ship docks at 6.30a.. We can disembark at 8.15.. Mom mentioned she'd like to go to Stonehenge.. I said that may be too much for you with the extra driving.. Other than that I don't know what there is to do in Southampton.. We won't know when to board again until we leave the boat.. Ship leaves at 5p so probably should be back at 4p..

Stonehenge completely threw me. I had imagined we would all take a walk around Southampton or drive somewhere nearby for lunch, allowing Fran and I to spend some time together afterwards. I quickly checked routes and options on my laptop.

Martin: I can be there by 8.30 no problem. I wasn't thinking of driving far tomorrow apart from back home afterwards, of course. Stonehenge is about an hour's drive each way. We'd have maybe a couple of hours there. Can we talk now or is that too expensive?

Fran: Can't call or chat until we dock.. These texts are costly too but it's what we have.. What could we do instead? Did you do any research about Southampton?

Martin: I looked for restaurants. I'll have to see if Stonehenge is doable. I don't really want the extra driving to be honest but it's OK.

Fran: Is there a cost for Stonehenge? I know they would be so happy to go there.. Mom doesn't get around all that well..

Martin: I understand. I'm not sure if you can get close to the stone circle itself, that's all. Entry to Stonehenge isn't too expensive. I'm going to go for a walk now, check out Southampton and where the terminal is.

I left the hotel in a foul mood. I was tired from my journey, and frustrated things were not going to plan. I found the cruise terminal easily, but had less luck locating the restaurants I had researched in advance. I found one, but it didn't look at all suitable. Another had closed for refurbishment. I bought coffee and a sandwich and sat in one of the city's parks to take stock of the situation. I sent Fran a text message.

I didn't find much for us to do here. It's all shops and bars. Maybe Stonehenge is best after all. I'm tired. OK. Here's the plan. I meet you at 8:30. We drive to Stonehenge. There's not a lot there other than the stones themselves, so we spend an hour or so there. If we need to eat, we can find a pub on the way back. We drop your parents back at the ship and if there's any time left you and I can go for a drink or something. I can't think of anything better.

I returned to the hotel resigned to the new plan, and desperately unhappy. I was aware my mood threatened to spoil the first—and perhaps only—time we would ever spend together. Sitting in my room, I resolved to let go of my expectations and allow things to happen as they would. Within minutes, my phone beeped. It was Fran.

Someone at dinner recommended Beaulieu motor museum.. It's closer I think.. I'm so excited.. I get to see you tomorrow! We'll figure it out..

I checked online. Beaulieu was only thirty minutes' drive from Southampton and there seemed plenty there for us to see and do.

Fran, that sounds a MUCH better idea! Let's do it! Good night. See you in the morning!

You're Shaking!

I set my clothes out for the morning, checked that my camera and satnav were charged, and tried to sleep. We had our day planned but I was still anxious. What if I was not allowed into the terminal to meet them from the ship? What if Fran's parents wanted to go to Stonehenge after all? What if we found ourselves awkward with each other? Fortunately, a close friend was online. She chatted with me for almost two hours. She reminded me the day would be a success, no matter what we did or what happened, because I would spend it in the company of my best friend. It was a powerful lesson in compassion and trust, and I am immensely grateful for her support.

I woke several times through the night. Each time, I checked the ship's position and webcam as she approached Southampton. She berthed on time, around half past six in the morning. I left the hotel shortly afterwards, and parked at the cruise terminal well ahead of schedule. All my frustrations and uncertainty melted away once I was there. I took photographs of the Queen Mary 2, and waited in the terminal building for Fran and her parents to come ashore. And then, all in a moment, they were there. Fran was there. Not three thousand miles away on webcam, but standing in front of me. We hugged across the barrier. My excitement must have been obvious, because Fran's first words to me were "You're shaking!"

Brayloo

Beaulieu (the name means beautiful place) is properly pronounced byoo–lee, but Fran mispronounced it as Brayloo, and insisted on calling it that for the rest of the day. The attraction—which includes Beaulieu Palace House, Beaulieu Abbey, and the National Motor Museum—opened at ten o'clock, which gave us plenty of time to get there. We stopped in the New Forest National Park to talk and exchange gifts. I also gave Fran the mobile wireless router, SIM cards, and printed instructions on which our ability to remain in touch might depend. We drove on to Beaulieu, and all enjoyed a drink together in the sunshine. After a while, Fran and I left her parents to explore at their own pace. I wrote later in my diary:

> We walked, and talked, and took photos of the Abbey and gardens, and went on the monorail and the old open-top bus, and walked some more, and sat, and talked some more. It was amazing—and the most natural thing in the world. If we were a little shy it didn't show. We were just two friends out together enjoying the day.

We dropped her parents back at the cruise terminal and went off on our own for a beer and what remained of our day together. All too soon, it was time to return Fran to the ship. I had imagined our parting might be emotional, but as we parked the car Fran told me she hated long goodbyes. Any tears could come later. I walked her to the terminal building. We hugged briefly, kissed, and with a wave she was gone. I would have liked to stay to watch the ship depart, but I had a seven-hour drive ahead of me. I texted "Bon voyage!" as I was about to set off. Her reply came back almost immediately.

Thank you for a lovely day.. It was so good to see you! Safe journey home!"

An hour or so later, as I was driving, my phone beeped again.

Tears.. I miss you..

Summary

In this chapter, we have seen how Fran and I navigated the five week period in May and June 2013, from the initial suggestion she might accompany her parents around Europe to our meeting face-to-face for the first time. We saw the trip as an opportunity as well as a challenge. Fran wanted to travel, to support and spend time with her parents, and to learn to trust her ability to look after herself. I saw it as an opportunity to confront codependency in our relationship. It took a great deal of hard work and sustained focus to get everything ready in so short a time, but we did so. The week-long transatlantic crossing and our meeting in Southampton brought their own challenges and rewards. Neither experience changed us fundamentally, but each in its way confirmed and validated the long distance, Internet-enabled friendship we had built throughout the previous two years.

In the next chapter, we see how we navigated the three months she was traveling around Europe.

9. A Hero's Journey: Sticking Together When Things Fall Apart

Just being willing to go into yourself is brave. Actually making the steps is a hero's journey.
—Fran Houston

"How Do You and Fran Get through Your Darkest Days?"

When things are at their worst, we focus on three basic principles: trust, challenge, and self-care. I could not support Fran at all if she did not want and trust me to do so. She trusts me not to hide or run away, and to hold a space in which she feels safe no matter how perilous her thoughts, feelings, and experiences might be. She also trusts me to handle my issues, so she can focus on hers.

We share a belief that even the most difficult experiences can yield rewards if we remain open to exploring them. The three months Fran spent in Europe were an immense challenge to her health and stability, yet she believed there was value to be gained from the experience. It could be argued she put her health—indeed her life—in danger by refusing to abandon the trip. There were times I argued for her to return home, but it was her choice to make. I would have supported her in either case. Stubborn persistence is part of Fran's makeup. Without it, she would not be who she is. Very probably, she would not be alive.

Extreme self-care becomes our guiding motto. We set minor matters aside and focus on whatever will best support her through the immediate crisis. Fran's wellness plan is invaluable at such times, as is our joint commitment to involve others when necessary. Paying close attention to my own health and well-being is no less important, and allows me to support Fran when she needs me the most.

Early Days and Places

Itinerary
We start each section by listing the places Fran and her parents stayed during that portion of their journey. The ongoing need to plan routes, accommodation, and places to visit contributed significantly to the stresses of the trip.

- June 10: Hardegsen (Germany)
- June 20: Scharbeutz
- June 25: Hardegsen
- June 30: Munich

Welcome to Germany
The *Queen Mary 2* took two days to reach Hamburg. Fran's final text message to me from the ship acknowledged the challenges ahead, but looked forward with acceptance and hope.

> Tomorrow I'll very much need your hand and heart.. We have many hoops to jump through.. Disembarking.. Taxi.. Rental car.. And journey south.. Whatever will be will be.. I will stay centered and calm and graceful..

They collected their rental car ("Everything fit.. Tightly, but it fit..") and drove to stay with relatives in Hardegsen. Fran settled in well. She was able to be herself, and found that people responded positively towards her. It was a joy for me to see her building on old relationships and developing new ones. Her relatives had Wi-Fi, which meant we could talk whenever we wanted, but it proved impossible to connect her parents' laptop to the Internet. This was intensely frustrating and a serious blow to our plans. We spent three days trying to resolve the issues before accepting defeat. The laptop remained unused for the rest of the trip.

Little had been planned in advance. The responsibility for researching routes and accommodation fell to Fran, but without the laptop she could only access the Internet on her mobile phone. I helped as much as I could, but stress soon began to affect her energy and mood. It was hard for her to maintain the healthy habits she relied upon at home. Most significantly, she had little privacy, physical space, or opportunity to meditate and rest. She slept poorly and developed a heavy cold. Things did not improve on a five-day visit to Scharbeutz, on the Baltic coast. There was no Wi-Fi in the apartment, and Fran's mobile wireless device failed to support voice calls. Within four days she had used almost all her data allowance for the month. There were bright moments, but her mood began to deteriorate sharply. On their return to Hardegsen, Fran found an envelope waiting for her.

> Thanks for your letter, Marty.. It's like being in the trenches.. getting letters from home..

My diary records that her mental health was starting to concern me, as was the suggestion she might be using alcohol as part of her coping strategy.

> Fran has drunk quite a lot tonight. As a one-off, that's fine, it might help her, but it is one more thing to keep an eye on, on top of some pretty unhealthy suicidal thinking.

Two days later, I added mania to my list of concerns.

> When we spoke this morning there was a distinct edge of mania in Fran's voice and manner of speaking, although she had also been drinking. She seemed calmer later on, so I am not really sure how she is. I was honest with her, though, and said I am detecting a manic edge.

I continued to research travel and accommodation options, and checked Fran's mobile phone account every morning so we could anticipate the cost of remaining in touch. She rarely felt she was coping well, and I did what I could to reassure and encourage her. Whenever she told me something the slightest bit positive or hopeful, I added it to a Good Moments list and e-mailed it to her so she had something to refer to when things were especially hard. I also struggled at times, especially early in the trip when we were coming to terms with our situation.

> We had a good phone call tonight. Fran offloaded about her day. I think it helped her to let go of the tension she was feeling. I wanted her to appreciate the things she has got right this past week, because she has done so well. Afterwards, she messaged me: "I'm glad we got to talk properly." I took the opportunity to mention we've not had chance to talk about my end of things. I've shared a few things about what I've been *doing*, but not about how I've been *feeling*. She said she's been stressed and under pressure and tired most of the time. I understand that. I don't need anything to change as such, but it helped that I got to say how I was feeling. It was exactly what we needed.

Surprise, Surprise

"I sent you an e-mail.. Surprise, surprise.." With those words Fran broke the news to me that her lease on the home she had rented for seven years would not be renewed at the end of October.

Martin: This just came through?

Fran: Yes.. This really sucks.. Where would I go?

Martin: I don't know. My first thought is you may need to return home, otherwise you're going to have next to zero time to find somewhere else to live.

Fran: I am pretty numb right now.. I've worked so hard to have stability and support.. Oh well.. Sigh..

Martin: It's because you have worked so hard that you are here at all. And I don't only mean here in Germany. I mean here at all. Alive at all. I want to say you are not alone, but I know that will ring pretty hollow right now. Hey, you could go live with your Mom.

Fran: Fuck you.. That's not even a joke..

Once over her initial shock, Fran handled things calmly and efficiently. Within a day she had spoken with friends back home, and exchanged e-mails with her care coordinator and housing agency. I was surprised and proud at how proactive she was, given all that was going on. She did precisely what was needed, and deferred any decision about returning earlier than planned.

The Road to Crisis

Itinerary

- July 2: Montafon (Austria)
- July 19: Augsburg (Germany)
- July 22: Erlenbach am Main
- July 26: Augsburg

The Friend She Needs Me to Be

Fran and her parents spent the next two and a half weeks in Montafon, in Austria. Their hotel had Wi-Fi, but it was difficult to synchronise our schedules for voice calls. We rarely managed more than fifteen minutes at a time, and went days without talking at all. About this time, Fran began talking about managing more on her own. ("I need to learn how to be myself and stay healthy, without you.") Although hard for me to hear, this was a healthy and necessary impulse. Writing my diary one evening, I recalled a favourite saying of ours: "Give people what they need, not what you need to give them."

> Fran has so much going on right now. I need to be here for her, but not push too hard or lay my own stuff on her too heavily. Now really isn't the time, with only chat and intermittent phone calls. I want to be the friend Fran needs me to be.

I had my own share of concerns, including work, family, and other friends who were struggling in various ways. If I was not to burden Fran with my problems, I needed to take responsibility for my self-care, and involve my wider support team if need be. I was still meditating daily and taking regular exercise. I began reading fiction and nonfiction titles on mental illness, and established a social media presence for our mental health work. Online and offline, I was talking more and more about our friendship, bipolar disorder, and mental health generally. I sometimes struggled to find time and energy for our book itself, but I gave myself permission to set that aside if necessary.

I've not done any writing in the past few days, but it's OK. Being there for Fran when she needs me is more important than writing about being there for Fran when she needs me.

We were learning parallel lessons about friendship, support, and codependency. Fran needed to focus on her own situation. This in no way relieved me of my responsibility to help where I could, but she needed me to trust; to trust her, to trust myself, and to trust the two of us to handle whatever arose.

Don't Hold Your Breath

Montafon provided a degree of stability, and Fran appeared to be adapting to being with her parents after years living on her own. Her most cherished moment of the summer came when she and her mother lay down on a bed of wild flowers in the Austrian Alps, "gazing at the sky and all around and singing German songs."

Today was a jewel.. it's what I came for.. few words exchanged but the magnitude of the outside matched the inside.. I believe we can continue staying in a better place.. we are communicating better..

She also took encouragement from being able to strike up meaningful relationships with people she met, and recalls one hotel worker with particular affection: "She was very supportive, understanding, and gracious to me." Nevertheless—and despite the occasional photographs she shared on social media which gave the impression she was enjoying herself—Fran was still struggling. Her normal coping strategies were founded on rest, personal space, and moderation in eating and drinking. These were all difficult to maintain when she was rarely out of her parents' company. She would later find the strength to demand personal space, but at this stage in the trip she accompanied them on almost all excursions and activities. To survive, she returned to the unhealthy coping strategies of the past. She overindulged with food, and was drinking as a means of getting through the day. She also resumed smoking. It was hard for me to witness.

Fran: 64.9 kg

Martin: Your weight? Hang on. That's 153 lbs. Ouch.

Fran: Fuck.. That's about a 10 lb gain in 6 weeks.. But no surprise.. I'm using food and drink to numb all this fucking pain and stress.. I was OK at first but I feel I've lost ground physically mentally and emotionally..

Martin: Can you contemplate changing that? Even small changes? If so, I will do all I can to help you. If not (and that is OK too, do what you need to do) then I will be here with you through it, and afterwards.

Fran: I really don't think I'd be doing so well if I didn't have alcohol to soften the blows.. I probably would have flown home already..

Martin: I understand. I don't have to like it, but you don't have to justify yourself to me.

Fran: I am medicating myself..

Martin: No. It is not medication. It is something to help you get through what is happening. That's OK, but we need to be clear about what's happening. Do you want me to help you monitor your drinking? I will ask you why you are putting yourself through all of this (and there is another seven weeks or so) if it's so bad now that you need to do these unhealthy things to get through it.

Fran: When else am I gonna get to do a trip like this? Yes it's fucking hard and I am doing things I rather wouldn't.. It's not comfortable like I would want.. But I will stay the course.. And no.. You don't get to monitor my drinking.. This trip may very well break me.. So be it.. At least we no longer have all you can drink and eat like it was on the ship.. That was kinda dangerous..

Martin: This is as real as it gets. I need you to know I am in your corner fighting along with you, not against you. It rips me to pieces to see you hurting like this, but I understand you need to be there. I will fight to keep you from harming yourself, but I can't take the hurt away and I need to let you do what you need to do.

Fran: Thanks.. I couldn't do any of this without you..

She was frequently depressed and suicidal.

Fran didn't leave the hotel today. She ate too much, and certainly drank too much. She got pretty low but we had a good phone call for an hour or so, after which she settled down to get some sleep. It's not just that things are bad right now. She cannot see much for her in the future either. She said, "I don't like how my life is going. Not one bit. I am to lose my home. I don't feel it's worth going on. What's the point? I had a career, a home, a future. Then I got sick. Now I have nothing. So what happens in my old age? I get to die alone. It is crazy for me to keep going." I told her, as I have told her many times, that I will always fight, tooth and nail, to keep her here. To keep her alive. She said not to hold my breath waiting for her to thank me.

Intervention

I was becoming increasingly concerned about Fran's mental and physical health. One day she had a serious argument with her mother. Fran's behaviour appeared extreme, but it was hard to gauge accurately because we had not been able to talk for three days. I felt we needed external, professional advice. I messaged her before I went to bed that night.

> I was reading your wellness plan today, where it says: "Let me know if you feel I am exhibiting any of these behaviours. I might not want to hear what you are saying so remind me of this document and that I asked you to help me take care of myself." I think we both agree you are depressed and having suicidal thoughts, and there is something close to self-harm with how you are drinking and smoking (and even that is not really helping things). You trust me to help you. I trust you to let me. I believe we need to escalate this. I've not been in touch with anyone else. Yet. But there are names on the wellness plan. They are there for a reason.

Next day, she drove to a nearby town. She needed time to herself, but messaged me from a bar. We chatted for a while, and then she told me she was going to have another beer. I said I did not want her to do that because she would be driving back later. I was unsure how she would react. I waited patiently. After a couple of minutes she replied.

Fran:	Hold my hand..
Martin:	I'm here. Did you read what I sent you last night?
Fran:	I don't know what to say or do.. I don't want to go home.. I really just want to step off the face of the earth.. Never to be seen again.. Vanish into thin air..
Martin:	This is why I wrote you what I did. We need to call in the troops.

There was another pause. I would have contacted her support team myself if necessary, but I wanted it to be a joint decision.

Fran:	Yeah.. OK.. Monday.. I don't have a clue what to say.. You know better than me..

Martin: I will work with you over these next few days, see how it goes, with a commitment from you to approach them on Monday if we still feel it is necessary. Tell me now if you are good with this, because I will hold you to it.

Fran: Yes Monday.. I'll have Wi-Fi.. And by then we can figure out what to say..

Martin: Thank you.

Fran appeared less stressed the next day. I wondered if I had acted hastily, or perhaps our conversation had jolted her into changing things. But there followed two really hard days which left me in no doubt we needed professional input to keep her safe. We each typed up our concerns and Fran e-mailed them out on Monday morning. Her psychiatrist responded almost immediately. He supported Fran resuming a low dose of risperidone to stabilise her mood, and suggested general coping strategies in line with her wellness plan. Her care coordinator offered a personal opinion that Fran should return home immediately: it was honest, but not particularly helpful.

Turning Things Around

Itinerary

- July 31: Rothenburg (Germany)
- August 2: Augsburg
- August 3: Füssen and Neuschwanstein
- August 4: Augsburg
- August 10: Göttingen
- August 11: Wolfsburg
- August 12: Bremen
- August 17: Cologne
- August 21: Oberhausen
- August 24: Amsterdam (The Netherlands)

An Angel in the Car

My role was to help Fran focus—and remain focused—on behaviours we knew could stabilise her. This included reminding her to shower every day, clean her teeth, and brush her hair each morning. As always, it only worked because Fran was prepared to work with me.

> Fran had a really tough day, but she stayed with me and allowed me to guide her. After breakfast she went back to her dorm at the hostel (after a cigarette with someone she met). She was full of disappointment and anger from yesterday. I let her do that for a while but I didn't want her to wallow, so I had her go out to a bookshop/coffee shop nearby to sit and write postcards. She then took a walk round the old town. She is in bed now and settling to sleep.

We chatted first thing each morning to discuss our plans for the day. This helped me assess how she was and check if she needed me to do anything for her. I continued to help plan routes and accommodation, and monitored her e-mail and social media accounts for anything she needed to address immediately. Occasionally, I could be of more practical assistance.

> Fran and co. went to Cologne Zoo today, and then drove to Oberhausen. That was interesting because they got lost and I ended up navigating them to the hotel. Fran said it was like having an angel in the car with them! It meant a lot to me too.

Fran was able to message me freely without being judged or criticised. ("I know I mercilessly dump on you what is going on, Marty, but you're my diary..") She also valued our calls—"It's so good to hear your voice"—though these depended on her having access to Wi-Fi and we sometimes went days without talking. Gradually, the change in medication and Fran's commitment to turning things around began to have an effect. She started having better days. Most important of all, she recognised she could influence how things went for the remainder of the trip.

I'm Finally on My Romp

> I have met a lot of beautiful people on this trip.. and a lot of mean people.. I am one.. I am both.. As are we all.. It's work.. It's hard.. But it's worth everything.. This thing called love.. Bloody messy thankless.. And sweet as hell.. This is a trip from hell.. A trip from heaven.. God damn my body hurts all over.. My neck and shoulders and back are excruciating.. I met some people today from Kansas living in India.. I really enjoyed talking to them.. I am so amazingly good at meeting strangers, connecting, exchanging information for possible future connection.. That's what I love most about traveling.. Even if I never see them again.. Knowing that we connected means everything to me..

That passage, written a few days after hearing back from her psychiatrist, reveals a great deal about Fran's health at the time. There was a distinct tang of mania, yet she could appreciate the joys of traveling and her ability to connect with others. This represented a significant shift in her thinking, which had previously been mired in her own situation. Three meetings were particularly significant. Two had been arranged in advance, but the first came completely out of the blue. Fran met her new friend in the Medieval Crime Museum in Rothenburg ob der Tauber. They connected immediately.

> We probably won't talk much the next couple of days. I'm finally on my romp. I met Pinky in the torture museum. We will go to Neuschwanstein together and stay overnight. She is full German but speaks not a word. I love her.

Fran's excitement and sudden change of plans struck me as distinctly manic, but she needed to change the dynamics of the trip and on balance this felt good to me. It was a time for me to stand back and allow her to do what she felt was right.

> I won't worry about you, Fran. I trust you. Check in with me when you feel a need to. This is a gift you have given yourself. I could not be more proud of you.

Fran updated me intermittently throughout the weekend. She was exhausted by the time she returned, but the break had clearly been good for her. A week later, she visited a friend who took her to see his friend's Arabian horses. They allowed her to experience sitting bareback on a rearing white stallion. When she caught up with me afterward she could scarcely contain her excitement.

> I am still processing my heart.. my first love.. Arabian horses.. Can't get my mind and heart around it.. I feel stunned and awed and scared.. Love and fear all intertwined..

Fran had also arranged to have lunch with an author friend who lived in Hamburg. She was looking forward to the excursion, but at the last minute her mother wanted to come along. Fran contacted me, frustrated and uncertain how to handle the situation.

> Frannie, I absolutely support your need to have today for yourself. Actually, never mind need. It's not always about what's needed or healthy. You're on vacation and have had very little chance to enjoy yourself. Whatever happens, I hope it works out OK.

Fran claimed the day for herself, and had a great time with her friend. She was making progress. The next few days went well. She messaged me early one morning, justifiably happy at the changes she had brought about.

Yesterday was so soul filling for me, Marty.. The best day yet.. Makes it all worth it.. This is what I came for.. I am proud of myself and the work I've done on myself, but I don't want that to end with the end of this trip..

Sadly, it was not to last. Within an hour, delight and pride turned to frustration as Fran struggled with her parents over their plans for the day. I did my best to stabilise her mood and thinking.

Fran: I have to bring my energy back.. I have none.. Get my mind around stuff.. I am so utterly wasted and shaky.. And I am burning up.. Disappearing..

Martin: You are flowing with words. That is OK up to a point, but also a possible mania flag.

Fran: Yeah.. i know.. i am sick.. physically and mentally.. not off the charts with mania yet.. but my body is way out of whack..

Martin: We need to be vigilant.

Fran: I am so fucking tired..

Martin: You were going to attempt some things from your to do list today, but maybe you need to rest first?

Fran: Yeah.. Maybe 30 mins shut eye would help..

Martin: Bring your focus in now, then. Rest.

Fran: OK..

Codependency and Coping

Fran's exhaustion and her need to take responsibility for herself meant we were less in touch than at any time since they arrived in Germany. The situation was compounded by technical issues and their frequent traveling.

Fran has been on the move again today. With all the driving and stress, and low battery on her phone, we haven't connected very well at all. I know she is fatigued and in a lot of pain, but it puts me on edge when we are not flowing. I guess I'm just feeling it more than usual.

Aside from feeling less able to help Fran, I needed support too. Many of the people in my life were struggling and I found it hard to balance my energies and attention. I felt adrift, confused, and lost. I found myself experiencing many of the symptoms of codependency, including feelings of abandonment, envy, and jealousy. Fran was not always able to help me, but we were never less than honest with each other.

Fran: It always takes you ages to say goodbye.. We're different like that.. I'm someone who likes to do it quickly.. So much drama.. I love it and not.. Makes me smile.. I don't like clingy and I like clingy..

Martin: OK.

Fran: I guess what I'm saying is sometimes I'm trying to go do something and we end up taking twenty minutes to say goodbye and then I resent that.. But I've never said anything because I don't want to hurt your feelings or for you to feel shunned..

Martin: I'm a bit fragile right now to process all this, but it's fine. You get to feel stuff, and to tell me how you feel. Then I get to feel stuff. It's all good. Don't feel you need to protect me though, I'm a big boy!

I e-mailed Fran later that day.

I understand that when we manage to get time (and technology) together you are often exhausted and in pain, and don't have energy or focus to stay on too long. That's OK. I've been feeling a bit fragile of late, and I guess that has come over as me being more clingy than usual. I try and stay level and positive, for myself and you and others. But it's hard sometimes. You are doing so well and I am proud of you. I know how difficult it is for you, and also what is up ahead. Other folk are having their hard times too. I'm trying to stay balanced. I have my wellness plan, but sometimes I need my best friend too.

It helped to share what I was feeling, but I needed other forms of self-care. I withdrew from social media for a time, and rededicated myself to my wellness plan. I meditated regularly, took evening walks, and read as widely as I could. Two books in particular affected me; *Through the Eyes of a Manic*, by Lesley Watson, and Patty Duke's *A Brilliant Madness: Living with Manic Depressive Illness*. Each deepened my awareness of what it means to live with illness. I also continued working on our book and expanded our presence on social media, building connections with groups and individuals in the mental health arena.

Graced with Newness

Anyone following Fran's social media posts would have imagined she was having the time of her life. That was far from the truth, but there were more and more glad moments and it was these Fran chose to share. The change in medication and her commitment to take time out for herself helped relieve the stress. Her suicidal thinking became less tormenting, and we kept her from sliding completely into mania. But risperidone and day trips were not enough on their own to get her through.

Martin: Tell me three things you want to accomplish today.

Fran: Charge my phone, smoke, breakfast, rest.. I will quit smoking on the boat home.. For now it helps take the edge off my stress..

Martin: That's four things. The cigarettes are self-medication for stress? Like drink is for mania and depression?

Fran: Yeah.. I'm using them now to make it through hell.. I need to smoke to give me a space to myself.. And to meet interesting normal people..

Martin: Interesting normal smokers.

Fran: It's either stuff myself with cigarettes and drink, or stuff myself with food..

Martin: Thank you. It helps me to understand. It isn't healthy but I'm not lecturing you. I get more concerned about the alcohol than food or cigarettes.

Fran knew I was not happy about how she was self-medicating, but she never hid it from me. One way or another, she moved through the days and weeks and places. On their final day in Germany, she posted an update to her social networking page.

I want to thank each and every one of you who has liked and commented on my posts these last months while I have been in Europe. It has not all been easy. It has stretched the limits of my ability to accept, love, and care. You have helped support and anchor me. I love traveling. It affords me the opportunity for constant learning and challenge. Each moment I am graced with newness and can choose to respond with acceptance and love . . . or not. It creates new synapses in my brain as I learn new ways of doing things and makes me stronger and more confident. Each city gives a new flavor of place and people. Traveling truly makes me savor each and every moment no matter what is happening around me. I leave for Amsterdam tomorrow and board ship next week. I'll be out of touch for over two weeks. See you when I get back. Tschüss!

Amsterdam

After all that had gone before, Fran was determined to enjoy Amsterdam on her own terms. She challenged her terror of getting lost ("I was petrified and fearful") and spent the first day exploring the city by train, tram, and boat. She lost her way a couple of times but handled things well.

Fran: Just missed tram 12.. Next in 15 minutes..
Martin: Shame you missed it, but never mind! You will have fun today.
Fran: It's all confusing to me.. I don't know how to read the maps.. I ask a lot of questions..
Martin: And it's a different language for you to deal with. This is courage.

. . . .

Fran: At the Rijksmuseum.. Gonna break then and go to van Gogh.. Then canal boat.. All around.. Then to Anne Frank maybe..

Martin: Well done for getting this far!

Fran: No beer here though..

Martin: It's only 11:30 am. You'll survive!

. . . .

Fran: There were long lines at van Gogh.. On Blue Boat Company canal cruise now..

Martin: I love exploring with you.

Fran: It's not simple, but I know how to get back..

. . . .

Fran: Off the boat.. Going to MOMO restaurant.. Then tram to the Hermitage museum..

Martin: You're doing so well!

Fran: Just trying to get my money's worth..

. . . .

Fran: I'm at the Aran Irish pub..

Martin: Hang on. I found the pub website. There's a 360 degree panorama of the inside. It looks amazing. Where are you sitting?

Fran: Five tables from the end.. Eating potato chips..

Martin: I'm eating a sandwich. Edam cheese in honour of Amsterdam! Are you enjoying the experience?

Fran: I'm still so stressed.. Hard to shake it.. My body hurts.. Hard to relax.. And am tired.. So maybe not really enjoying, but I am aware of how I am..

Martin: I guess I was being a little optimistic. But you feel satisfied with how you are handling yourself today?

Fran: Been basically zooming through the museums..
          Usually art is relaxing to me.. But I find I'm
          somewhat disinterested.. But I am glad about
          managing the trams and map stuff.. Didn't do it
          perfectly.. But am getting it..

The second day in Amsterdam—the last of their European tour—passed easily. We spoke briefly in the evening. Our plans to have a beer together never materialised, but I drank one while writing my diary.

Tomorrow Fran boards ship for the two week cruise back to New York. We probably won't be in touch much: perhaps a chat here and there when they dock. It's been an incredible summer, for Fran and for our friendship. Here's to you, Fran! Here's to us! Safe journey home!

Using the Darktime

Itinerary
This section covers the two-week cruise from Amsterdam to New York aboard the MS *Eurodam*, and Fran's final few days before returning home.

- August 27: Set sail from Amsterdam
- August 29: Stavanger (Norway)
- August 30: Bergen (Norway)
- September 2: Reykjavik (Iceland)
- September 6: Nanortalik (Greenland)
- September 8: St John's (Newfoundland)
- September 10: Halifax (Canada)
- September 12: New York (US)
- September 16: Home

You Help Me Beat My Depression

Our first opportunity to connect properly was in Reykjavik, five days into the cruise. Fran was desperately fatigued, and in emotional and physical pain. She was relieved to have made it through the summer but fearful of the future. We had always known the summer would be hard, but instead of recuperating she faced finding somewhere to live, packing, leaving her community, and settling into somewhere new. It was not merely daunting, it was potentially dangerous.

Fran: I've missed you..

Martin: I've missed you too.

Fran: You help me beat my depression..

Mary: That's because I come down there to find you, in the darkness where you are. I sit with you until you are ready to walk out again into the sunlight.

Fran: From this bleak harsh landscape..

Martin: Iceland?

Fran: Yes..

Martin: The landscape can be an analogy for your depression. Let's use this part of the journey, this Darktime. Feel the sadness, and then leave it behind on these shores.

Fran: I don't like this part of the trip.. Coming home.. It's scary..

Martin: Find me a stronger word than scary.

Fran: Terrifying..

Martin: Good. If it's terrifying then say so. Feel it fully. Because if you can feel it, it will keep you from falling deeper into depression.

Fran: I haven't made the most of Norway and Iceland.. I don't like them.. They are not warm like Germany..

Martin: On the way back to the ship, find me one thing that delights you. A smile. A ray of sunlight. Anything.

She messaged me later.

Fran: We sail soon..
Martin: What did you find for me?
Fran: The bus driver.. And a woman named Cindy who went to buy a swimsuit..
Martin: As you found two things I will ask for three tomorrow.
Fran: The blue of the water.. The brown of Mum's eye.. The niceness of people caring for us..
Martin: I said tomorrow! That's cheating! (Thank you.)

They were at sea for the next four days. We were able to chat when they reached Nanortalik in Greenland, and I was relieved to discover her mood had lifted a little. I didn't expect us to be in touch again until they landed in Newfoundland, but some personal news required me to contact Fran the next day. Despite the cost, we exchanged text messages throughout that day and for the remainder of the cruise. It helped Fran process her feelings from the summer and prepare for all she would face once she returned home. She was by turns angry, tearful, and depressed. Most of all, she was exhausted. One bright moment occurred as they reached Halifax, Nova Scotia. I was at work, and a colleague found a webcam that showed the *Eurodam* as it berthed at the ferry terminal.

Martin: Frannie, I have the ship on webcam! I watched you coming in. The camera is looking down on the ship from outside the terminal.
Fran: Would you see me if I waved?
Martin: Maybe! Are you at a window?
Fran: I could go up top on the back deck..
Martin: Yes do! Let me know when you get there!
Fran: OK.. I'm by the stacks..
Martin: I think I can see you! Walk about a bit.
Fran: I'm right by the railing..

Martin: Yes! I can see you! I am waving!
Fran: Can you see my big belly?
Martin: Haha! No but I can see you!
Fran: I'm going back down now.. I don't have a coat and it's cold..
Martin: Go and warm yourself up! I can't believe I just saw you on webcam from all the way over here!
Fran: That was awesome.. Thank you for doing it with me..
Martin: Thank Barry, he found the webcam!
Fran: Thank you, Barry!

I took a screenshot of Fran waving, and shared it on our social media pages. A little later she went ashore and we were able to talk. The call only lasted a few minutes, but it was our first since Amsterdam and helped us feel connected again.

An Ending and a Beginning
The next day was their final full day at sea. It was also the twelfth anniversary of the 9/11 attacks in New York City and Washington, D.C. Fran was calm through most of the day, but by evening she became stressed, angry, and exhausted. They went for dinner ("I drank champagne and told them we were toasting you.") and then Fran moved to the bar, leaving her parents to finish their packing.

Fran: Everyone around us is hugging.. Too bad I can't even find a good looking guy to spend the night with so I don't have to go back to the cabin.. My life sucks.. I deserve better.. I have a wicked headache.. And am wicked tired.. And I can't go to sleep because they are packing..
Martin: You have achieved something remarkable these past months. If you'd known how it would be you never would have gone. I never would have let you. You dared to put yourself out there. You kept going. You never gave up. This is once in a lifetime stuff.

Fran:	I'm scared of the next few days.. It will be hell..
Martin:	I'm sorry it ends this way. Will you please go back to your cabin? Tell them I said they must let you rest, so you can be safe. For me, please.
Fran:	I'm having a beer now.. So many normal people here doing normal things.. I'd like to be like that..
Martin:	Drink a toast to yourself, by all means, or to me, or to the end of the summer. But don't drink to smother the pain. There's not enough booze on the ship for that. Getting drunk is "normal" but it isn't good for you when you are so depressed.
Fran:	I'm not planning to get drunk.. It gives me a headache anyway.. Just want some peace and some sleep.. I wanted to give them some space to pack.. I'm sure they blame me for all the stress..
Martin:	Maybe. I'm the lucky one. I get to chat with you at three in the morning! You get to smile at Marty for being . . . well, for being Marty!
Fran:	Shall I let you sleep? I am smiling..
Martin:	I will stay a little longer. You don't need to keep texting me, but I'd like one later so I know you are back in your cabin.
Fran:	Should I try to go back now? Beer's done.. Everyone's cleaning up.. I'm beat.. Jeez I've used a lot of texts.. They'll be expensive..
Martin:	Yes. It's time for you to go to bed.
Fran:	Night night..

Dry Land

The *Eurodam* arrived in New York early next morning. Fran spent four days at her parents' house before flying home. We were able to message, talk, and have video calls again, but it was a difficult time. The summer had taken an extraordinary toll on her mental and physical health. The effort it had taken her to fight through to the end had protected her to some degree. Now there seemed little reason for her to go on.

Fran is still at her Mom's, and seriously depressed. She is as down as I've ever known her. She has spoken several times of wanting to be dead, of wanting to die. It got pretty real. Hopelessness and helplessness, and a sort of angry, vengeful, suicidal thinking that's new and feels dangerous. She said I'd be better off if I'd never met her, because then I wouldn't have the pain of being her friend.

The day finally dawned for her return home. She messaged me from the airport lounge.

Fran: Thanks for watching over me..
Martin: You're welcome.
Fran: I mean it.. I would not be alive without you.. Wherever I go.. there you are.. However I am.. you accept or gently challenge.. Whatever I do.. You cheer me on.. You are the bestest friend I could ever have..
Martin: We are here for each other.
Fran: I gotta go.. Boarding..
Martin: Take care. We did good. You did good.

Summary

The three month driving tour through Germany, Austria, and the Netherlands was also a journey of self-discovery. The trip was far more demanding than anticipated, and brought Fran to the point of mental and physical collapse. It was important for me to pay attention to my own well-being. As Fran's single point of support, I provided continuity and structure when everything else was chaotic, stressful, and increasingly dangerous. We used many of the techniques described in earlier chapters, and called on professional support when it was clear we needed to. Fran made it home depressed and exhausted, but intact. In the next chapter, we see how Fran faced the challenge of finding somewhere to live, moving home, and beginning a new life in the city.

10. A Life worth Living: Hope in Unexpected Places

You've helped me make a life worth living.
Thank you.
—Fran Houston

"Why Do You Do It?"

People are sometimes surprised how much time Fran and I spend together, and the degree of support I provide. One friend commented, "Realistically, who's got the time and energy to unfalteringly provide that level of care and dedication to someone outside your immediate family?" It is a valid question, but misses the point a little. Not everyone with mental illness wants or needs the kind of caregiving relationship that works for us. What they almost certainly do want and need are friends they can rely on. Why is that so important? We all need support and companionship, but people living with mental illness often find friends are in short supply. Changes in mood, energy, and behaviour can strain relationships and leave people isolated precisely when they need help the most. Be the friend who doesn't walk away when things get rough. It is not always easy for us either, but what began as a private joke captures the essence of commitment.

"You're stuck with me now, Frannie. I hope you realise that."

"Like gum on my shoe."

Someone wrote to us recently, "Your journey as friends reminds us that mental illness doesn't change what friendship is all about: being there for those we love." That meant a lot because the reciprocal nature of our relationship is not always recognised. Fran is there for me as much as I am there for her.

204

She is neither a drain on me nor a burden—although she doubts this on occasion.

> Fran said to me today, "I don't get it. Why are you still here?" I told her no matter what is going on, whether she is having a good day or a bad day, whether I am having a good day or a bad day, I never don't want to be here.

I am a better person for knowing Fran. I have a greater understanding of my strengths, values, weaknesses, and vulnerabilities than ever before. I have learned more about mental and invisible illness, suicidal thinking, stigma, determination, courage, and responsibility since we became friends than in the fifty years before we met. I have explored meditation, Non-violent Communication (NVC), mindfulness, and other techniques that benefit my life enormously. I have greatly expanded my circle of friends, met people who feel safe sharing their stories in response to mine, and learned how it feels to offer my skills and experience in the service of others. I have grown—and continue to grow—as a friend and as a man. But the most important thing I have gained is our friendship itself. Why do I do it? Because Fran is my best friend and that is what best friends do.

A Little Boat in a Big Ocean

We always knew the summer would be an immense challenge for Fran, and anticipated an extended period of rest and recuperation afterwards. Instead, she returned from Europe needing to find a new home, pack up her belongings, and move from the little house she had lived in for seven years. My role was to keep an eye on her physical, emotional, and mental health; help her stay as stable as possible; and keep her moving with all she needed to do. I imagined she would need at least a few days' rest, but she immediately set to work. She contacted her landlord and began checking her housing and other benefits. She also listed the key features she was looking for in her next home.

Location: Portland (West End or East End), access to grocery shopping, gym, medical appointments, off-road parking.

Neighbourhood: quiet, public transportation.

Features: bathtub and shower, living room, bedroom, office, storage, futon for visitors, air-conditioning, ground floor or not many stairs, outside space (balcony or garden), able to entertain (spacious, nice, proud to call my home).

This was more than a shopping list. Her choices displayed an understanding of what she would need to keep well and stable, also the belief she deserved somewhere nice to live and—crucially, given her recent suicidal ideation—had a future to plan for. She arranged the first apartment viewing within days of arriving home. I helped as much as possible. I established a shared online area to hold the lists and spreadsheets we would need for property searches, and helped edit e-mails and letters. I also helped her process the summer's events by organising the hundreds of photographs she had taken in Europe. We had a lot to think about.

Fran: The first thing is find out whether I get to keep all my services..

Martin: It is Friday today. I'm guessing you won't hear back about that over the weekend. But we can work on your strategy and to do list in the meantime.

Fran: Yes.. Good idea.. I need you to bounce ideas back and forth..

Martin: I need to be careful not to try and step in and take over. I don't know enough about things over there to do that. But I want to be as involved as you want me to be. We are a team.

Fran: I am so very glad and thankful I have you in my life holding my hand.. I would be utterly lonely and distraught without you.. Thank you..

Island life had not always been easy for Fran, but it had provided structure and a degree of stability. In particular, the stretch of water separating her from the mainland had provided a natural boundary that buffered her from the outside world.

Fran: If i move i will have to create inner boundaries rather than having external ones to protect me.. i guess most of my pain comes from holding on..

Martin: So much of what we do is about letting go, isn't it? The body letting go of weight, letting go of emotions once we have acknowledged them. The letting go of thoughts and bodily sensations in meditation.

Fran: When i talked to my psychiatrist the other day i said how things would be very different if i didn't have your care and support in my life.. i'm very aware how i teeter and totter and you help guide me to my center, and remind me who i am..

Martin: We are important to each other, for sure. Sometimes we ponder our levels of codependency, and it's good that we do so. We are both aware of the dangers. I think it's healthy that we are able to adapt to change. That's what we did over the summer. It's what we are doing now.

Fran: I'm trying to find where I belong, and a life that fits me.. I hope somewhere does.. I hope I find my tribe.. People who make sense to me.. This island no longer fits..

Martin: This is an important moment. It is not easy to grow. You have more courage than anyone I have ever known.

Fran: People don't do what I do?

Martin: The inner work? Few ever attempt that.

Fran: Really? I really don't know what I'm doing..

Martin: That may be the wisest thing you've ever said! But you never give in. You never give up. Just don't go getting the idea you're perfect or anything.

Fran: I'm a little boat in a big ocean..
Martin: Sail, little boat.
Fran: Hold my string..
Martin: I am. I will.

I Do Not Give You Permission to Give Up

At the time, I was writing what would become chapter 7 of this book, about suicide and suicidal thinking. To build on what I already knew I took several online courses and read as widely as I could.

Martin: I just bought three books. Two are about bipolar disorder, the other one is about suicide awareness.
Fran: You are a crazy cat for studying bipolar me..

Of course, no matter how many books I read and how many classes I completed, I could not make Fran's illnesses go away. My role was to help her stay as stable and healthy as possible, as part of her wider support team. Fran attended appointments with her psychiatrist, doctor, and care coordinator as soon as possible.

Martin: Did your appointment with your psychiatrist go well?
Fran: Yes. I told him of your support on the trip.. He asked how it went meeting with you in Southampton.. I said you were like a big lovable golden retriever with a heart of gold.. My golden, Bo, was my soulmate..
Martin: That moves me deeply, Frannie. Thank you.

Living with illness has given Fran a stubborn resilience and the ability to direct her often limited resources where they are most needed. When she first learned the lease would expire on her home, she was three and half thousand miles away in Europe. The prospect alarmed her, but after confirming the details she put the matter aside to focus on making it through the summer. By the time she returned she had regained half the weight she had worked so hard to lose over the previous year. Her weight disgusted her, but she had more pressing concerns and brought her energies to bear on finding a new home. We worked hard day after day, and also set time aside to relax, meditate, and review Fran's photographs from the summer. Things eased for a while, especially when she felt she was making progress, but fatigue and stress gradually took hold again. By the end of September she described herself as "tired, tetchy, and emotional."

Fran: i'm a fat cow.. i feel so squirmy.. not myself at all.. i feel under pressure.. i feel invalidated by the universe.. it doesn't make any sense.. how i feel.. i want to be left alone.. i want everything to already be done.. i don't want the process.. even though it could be lovely.. i probably won't let it be..

Martin: I'm not sure it has to make sense, Fran. Illness is illness. But it is understandable, given what you have gone through and are going through now.

Fran: it's hard for me to feel like i deserve anything good.. especially when opportunities are not opening up.. but the worse thing is.. i feel like i wanna push you away..

Martin: That is new, and potentially dangerous. But I am here to tell you, I'm not going anywhere.

Despite my best efforts, she slipped deeper and deeper into a mixed state of depression, anxiety, and incipient mania. We knew better than to ignore the signs.

Martin: I can feel how hard you are finding all this. It is close to overwhelming.

Fran: i'm tired.. trouble focusing.. i ate.. maybe now shower? i think i'm depressssssssed..

Martin: I think so too. All the "it's not working" talk you've been doing is a sign of that. But there are some elements of mania in there too. Would you agree?

Fran: yes.. for sure.. my life seems to be moving out from

> under me.. i wanna give up.. it's too hard..
>
> Martin: I know. But I do NOT give you permission to give up. You have done so much since you got back.
>
> Fran: there are so many things i haven't done..
>
> Martin: Then we prioritise them. And if there are things other people can help with, we call them in.

Things were becoming increasingly hard for her to deal with. More than once she declared this would be a particularly good time for suicide because it would save her from having to face the upheaval, loss, and uncertainty that lay ahead. Her weight continued to rise sharply. This added to her depression and self-disgust, but there was no point suggesting healthier strategies. Every resource she had was devoted to survival.

> Martin: Over the summer you used food to self-medicate. You were aware you were doing that, and it is part of what got you through the trip. Is that what's happening now?
>
> Fran: i think it's stress.. i'm eating and drinking to counteract that.. to numb my feelings of homelessness instead of healing them..

You'd Be Fine without Me

On the eve of Fran's birthday we met for our usual video call. She opened the birthday card and gifts I had sent her, but we also touched on deeper issues, including her suicidal thinking.

> I'm not sure how to describe how it is when we're talking like that. I am calm. Mostly we are both calm. I guess because it usually happens when Fran is deeply depressed. But we do not skirt around things. Last night Fran was talking about how she still has a stash of tablets put aside. We also talked about how she once promised her psychiatrist she wouldn't try and kill herself without calling him first. And how, if she ever did attempt suicide and

failed, she would carry that stigma always. We are both aware that this is very real. But it wasn't desperate or panicky. It was genuine and open and honest. I had not the slightest worry about leaving her when it came time to part at 2 a.m.

The following conversation took place a few days later, in the early hours of the morning.

Fran: you'd be fine without me..

Martin: Fuck that.

Fran: didn't mean to piss you off!

Martin: I know. It just sounded just a bit too much like "you'd be better off without me messing your life up."

Fran: i'm in a bad way.. i feel responsible for you.. like you need me..

Martin: If that keeps you here, then good. This is as deep and dark a time as I've ever known with you. I won't pretend otherwise.

Fran: the alcohol helps..

Martin: It helps suppress it?

Fran: it numbs me and makes me happy.. things don't matter so much.. it would be so much easier if i checked out before i move.. i can't imagine the city being better than here..

Martin: You can't imagine it because you cannot see anything good at all from inside this depression. That is precisely why you need to try and stop the drinking. I should have realised sooner. You have a home to find and move into, and trips to plan, and the world tour for our book to arrange.

Fran: hahahahahaha.. i am laughing out loud.. you are a crazy cat.. i wish everyone had a marty.. you make everything better..

Martin: Haha!

Fran:	i did good today going to view those places.. spontaneously..
Martin:	Yes you did.
Fran:	so i'm not a complete smuck..
Martin:	Not a complete one, no.

Can't You Just Fix me?

Depression and suicidal ideation were not the only things Fran had to deal with. By now, we both recognised that mania had taken hold.

Fran:	i'm hanging onto the bed.. i feel so crazy.. racing thoughts.. stuff to do.. racing mind lots of dreams.. i've been very stimulated this week.. feels like i've been holding on for 4 months and now i can fall apart..
Martin:	Does it taste of mania?
Fran:	i think so.. i'm all over the place.. gotta get back to meditating and my wellness plan..
Martin:	Is it worth a call to your psychiatrist about your meds?
Fran:	think we should wait see if it passes.. wanna see if i can manage on my own..
Martin:	OK, but remember it's not a sign of weakness to use meds when you need them. They are a tool in the toolbox. Your safety is the number one priority. When you are OK (stable) then everything else falls into place. It's my job to keep us focused on that. Any time I forget, you have my permission to slap me!
Fran:	don't worry i will..

She was also sleeping poorly, and after a week or so she took an extra dose of risperidone to help calm herself down. I had no particular concerns—Fran always treats medicines with respect—but I suggested she consult her psychiatrist before doing so again.

Fran: i took a risperdal last night because my mind is racing and i'm anxious.. i feel a lot of pressure.. too much going on.. overwhelmed.. even if it might be good things.. it's frightening.. i can't even count to 20 and back with my breathing.. i get distracted by my thoughts..

Martin: I hear you. This tends to happen when you have a couple of days of good progress. I'm here to be your anchor. Let the thoughts come and go without holding on to them too much. They are just thoughts, they are not you. Risperdal is part of the toolkit.

Fran: i'm glad you didn't yell at me, for taking it without asking you.. my doc and i talked about staying on it through the moving.. i take it at night.. this morning i took an additional one..

Martin: I trust you. But if you feel you will need to do this again, check with him first, OK?

Fran: OK.. gonna meditate now or try to..

Supporting Fran means paying attention to her needs and not assuming I know best. This can be as simple as asking, "What do you need most right now?" When I asked one day, she gave me the analogy of a sieve: "The good stuff runs through and constantly needs topping up.. What sticks are all the negative ones.." She needed me to keep the sieve topped up by reminding her—over and over, where necessary—of her achievements, and reassuring her she was not alone.

Today I've helped Fran focus on her bills and paperwork. It was a slog for her, but I thanked her when we got together later because she did her best and didn't fight me all the way. She has so much still to do, but she is doing it.

It was hard going at times. One day it took all my powers of persuasion to walk her to the bathroom to take a shower. My relentless optimism—what Fran calls my pathological positivity—irritated her, but I could use the energy of irritation to stir her into movement.

Fran: dammit.. this day sucks.. even if it is gorgeousity.. it still sucks.. my problem is fundamental non acceptance.. i don't like how anything is..

Martin: Do a quick loving kindness meditation. You know how it goes. May I be well. May I be happy. May I be peaceful. May I be loved. May you be well. May you be happy. May you be peaceful. May you be loved.

Fran: damn you.. can't you just fix me? why do i have to do the work.. it's everyone else, not me..

Martin: There is no everyone else, Fran. You have my support, always. But yes, you have to do the work. What's next on the agenda?

It was fortunate other friends were able to support Fran in ways I could not from three thousand miles away. Some helped declutter her home and pack things she wanted to take with her. One friend helped organise a yard sale to sell items she no longer needed. Another drove her to view potential properties. Fran was grateful, but found it hard to reenter relationships after a summer away. It particularly distressed her that some people failed to grasp the nature of her conditions.

Some don't believe in illness.. which is dangerous to me.. they think i can talk myself out of it.. it's true i can shift things a little.. away from mania.. or depression.. but i cannot control it.. i can only manage.. with meds and support.. someone telling me they can't see me as ill doesn't help me.. you're the only one who has taken the time to know me and my illnesses.. others don't want to connect with the illness part..

No Longer an Islander

Contrary to all expectations, it took only a little over three weeks for Fran to find somewhere suitable to live. There was no disguising her excitement.

Fran: I have an apartment!

Martin: Wow! How do you feel?

Fran: I feel good.. My mouth is smiling.. I feel light.. Energetically it feels good..

Martin: This is big! A new home! I know it's not all going to be smiles and sunshine and there is still a lot to do. But I'm so proud of you!

Her mood lifted almost immediately. She became less agitated and accomplished tasks calmly and methodically. She looked ahead to her new life with hope.

Fran: I will make a good nourishing comfortable mature fun home for myself..

Martin: You are on the right track now, Fran. This summer, as hellish as it was at times, gave you the strength and purpose to do these things. You discovered you can do this stuff. This life stuff. You won't live to regret this. You will be too busy LIVING to look back with regret.

She had secured an apartment but there was a great deal to be done and the future remained uncertain and scary. Doubts crept back in, bringing with them a sense of hopelessness and desperation. She felt under pressure to suppress what she was feeling so as not to distress or alarm others.

Fran: i feel like crying.. end of an era.. don't know what the next one will bring.. a separation from my home, my island, my tribe.. thrown into the hectic city life..

craziness, busyness, strangers.. i am no longer an islander.. i am a flatlander.. a portlander.. almost.. but I have to lie to everyone and say i'm happy..

Martin: Not to me.

Fran: no.. i can always be my true self with you..

Martin: There will be things you love about your new life. Some you hate. Some will just be different. You are facing so many changes. Much of the pattern and structure that have been part of your life for years is going to change. Is that part of what you are feeling?

Fran: i felt like i was building something before summer came.. and now it's all gone to shit.. and i won't be able to get it back..

Martin: The way I see it, you were building your life in very positive ways. You had a big timeout over the summer, and now there is this move to deal with. But you will pick up again. This would be so much harder if you had not done all that work before.

Fran: ahh.. that is true.. i would have checked out already..

Martin: Not if I had anything to do with it!

Fran: i can't imagine my life without you.. it would be dark, bleak, hopeless..

Letting Go

It would be wrong to imagine that I always got things right, especially concerning Fran's relationship with food and drink. Her weight continued to rise. This affected her mood, but she seemed to refuse responsibility for what she ate and drank. Things came to a head one evening when I insisted on discussing her eating habits. It was the last thing Fran wanted to do. Within moments she became frustrated and angry. I felt responsible for pushing ahead and not picking up the signs. We ended the call early, without resolving our differences. She phoned a friend who was able to calm her, and suggested delaying work on her weight until after the move. Fran and I exchanged a few chat messages but I was still feeling dreadful when I wrote my diary.

I have to accept she's not ready to face cutting back right now. I asked if we'd webcam later tonight. She said she needed space to do stuff. I'm not sure if she meant until we meet at 11 p.m. or if she can't face more of me tonight. I'd intended doing more work on the book, but how can I write about being there for her when I just messed up like this?

I messaged her later to say goodnight. She replied immediately, "Nooooooo! I'm eating right now but I wanted to meet. Are you too exhausted? What do you need?" Her attention to my needs after what had happened moved me deeply. We met for our video call as usual. We were cautious, but did not try to ignore or dismiss what had happened. It was a great example of feeling, acknowledging, exploring, and letting go of our hurts without blaming each other for them.

There came at last a period of calm in which Fran was able to set aside her worries and apply herself mindfully to the tasks at hand. It was a joy to witness.

i'm learning to be gentle with myself by doing a little bit at a time and by changing my attitude about everything being so hard.. it actually can be ok.. or even enjoyable.. letting go can be enjoyable.. it doesn't have to be a loss.. i need not hold onto the old.. that hasn't worked very well.. being gentle with myself is honoring myself.. i'm learning to have a good relationship with myself..

After decades of self-doubt, she was starting to believe herself worthy of a home and a life she could feel proud of.

i know how i want my new home to be.. sparse.. that will be better for my mind.. it is so satisfying to have a clean home.. uncluttered.. it makes me feel so much better..

I helped when asked, but otherwise allowed Fran to get on with what needed to be done. This worked well for us both. She even found time to work with me on the book, and we signed up for a new meditation course.

Surprisingly Calm and Trusting

The day before her move, Fran collected a rental truck and took it across to the island on the ferry. She had never driven anything as large before and it brought her justifiable pride. I asked how she felt. "I'm surprisingly calm and trusting. I'm learning to not have drama and chaos in my life. To be gentle, kind, and thoughtful instead.."

She had arranged for friends to help with the move itself. We chatted early in the morning before they arrived. The next time I heard from Fran, she was in the truck queuing for the ferry.

Fran:	On the boat line for the 10am boat..
Martin:	Wow! You guys did well to be loaded up so quickly!
Fran:	It took only 2 hours.. Friends gave me Brut champagne.. I just sent you my position..
Martin:	I have you. Here we go! Bye bye to the island. Hello to the new you!

I tracked her online as she crossed to the mainland, and then as she drove to her apartment. She messaged me the moment she arrived.

Fran:	Can you see me?
Martin:	Yes! I followed you all the way. Welcome home!

Building My Life from the Ground Up

Portland brought the promise of stability after months of challenge and stress, but it took time for us to adjust to the rhythms of city life.

A Very Different Pulse

Fran had a new life to settle into and a new city to explore. For the first time in months, she was free to do things for herself. Independence was healthy, but it was difficult for me to adjust after months of being closely involved in all she was doing. The structure of our days—the times we chatted, talked, and had our video calls—had evolved when she lived on the island and came to town once or twice a week, mostly to attend medical appointments. She now lived in the middle of a bustling, vibrant city and felt restricted by the need to meet at our normal times when there was so much to do, see, and explore. Other friends also wanted to connect. She found it hard to balance the conflicting demands on her time. I found it hard accepting that Fran was content for us to spend less time together, and envied those she spent more time with. I wanted to be involved in her life as fully as possible. Fran wanted to share it with me, but on her terms. These were classic symptoms of codependency, and it did not take us long to notice what was happening. What Fran needed most of all was space, and for me not to put additional pressure on her. We were honest and open about what we were experiencing—"Our lives have a very different pulse now that you are on the mainland."—and we resolved to move forward gently, respecting each other's needs.

> Fran was really tired when we met last night, but that led to us having a really easy time. We did another of the meditations which brought us up to date. I wrote up my notes from the session while Fran rested (she wrote hers up today) and then talked a while, including about when we met in Southampton. We didn't touch on anything contentious or too challenging. We talked about how nice it is to do that sometimes.

We still met most days, but I was learning to accept she would sometimes choose to do things without me, or meet other people during "Marty time." It was an important lesson in trust, and a powerful antidote to codependency. Gradually, new patterns emerged. Fran's first priority was settling into her new home. I helped her choose furniture, and a laptop to replace her ageing computer. This went deeper than simply buying new things. For almost the first time in Fran's life, she felt herself worthy of living well.

> i want to make choices i don't have to undo.. or have to live with and make due.. i want to love everything that is in my home.. and if it's not just right i can let it go.. i want to stop making do, scrimping, undeserving mindsets.. this is a way of loving myself.. valuing myself.. caring for myself.. it really does feel better than keeping socks with holes in them..

It meant a great deal to Fran that I was there to share the experience and decision-making. We updated our shared calendar, pencilling in appointments, events, and activities for the days and weeks ahead. It helped us to visualise the likely shape of things to come, but we were careful not to hold too tightly to the new schedule. It was important to allow room for growth and change. Using all the techniques at our disposal, I accompanied Fran as she explored her neighbourhood. In a delightful echo of Halifax, Nova Scotia, we discovered there was a public webcam overlooking the Christmas tree in the centre of town.

Fran: go to the website, click on the main street monument square webcam.. i'll message you when i am at the tree.. about 20 minutes..
Martin: Cool!
Fran: i'm here now.. in front of the white truck..
Martin: Is that you waving?
Fran: yes!
Martin: I see you! This is fun! I took a screenshot for old times' sake!

I'm Never Giving up on You

In late November, Fran took a short trip with a friend to the Kripalu Center for Yoga and Health in Stockbridge, Massachusetts. They left on Thanksgiving Day, and Fran thanked me for making such a difference in her life. We both had tears in our eyes. I reprised my "angel in the car" role by helping them navigate to their hotel.

> I had just come off the computer when Fran messaged me "HELP!" because they were getting close to Kripalu and weren't sure of the route. So I turned the PC back on, found and messaged her the directions, and then went to bed!

The workshop was challenging, but Fran connected well with the people she met. I wrote in my diary, "She's found some real insights on this trip. It is so good to see how much she is growing." It was a brief respite. Within days of returning things were hard again. My diary is full of words like "anxious," "tired," "frazzled," "stress," and "depressed." She seemed overwhelmed by her new life and doubted herself at every turn.

Fran:	i feel pretty flat and exhausted.. i'm scared to death of homemaking.. i don't know how to do it.. there are so many choices.. it's really hard for me.. i don't have any of the skills..
Martin:	You are still finding your way, Fran. It is three weeks tomorrow since you moved in. Look at what you've achieved! Sure, there are boxes you've not unpacked. But you've had visitors. You have a sofa on order, and a new laptop. You have cleaned. You have set fire to the microwave! You've explored some of the neighbourhood, been to the cinema, met up with friends, and had a long weekend away. I'm so proud of you!
Fran:	it's a good thing i have you to remember all of it.. i don't give myself a break..

She was physically and mentally exhausted, and barely functioning. I encouraged her to rest when she could. Sometimes, I sat quietly with her while she tried to sleep. Most important of all, I made sure she knew I wasn't going anywhere.

Fran: i feel like i'm losing it..

Martin: You feel overwhelmed by everything you feel you have to do? The pace of the city?

Fran: yeah.. and depressed.. and tired..

Martin: I am never letting go of this end of the string, Fran. I am never giving up on you.

Fran: Good luck with that..

Somebody Has to Get Me Ready

Gradually, Fran began moving forward again. She attended appointments with her psychiatrist and care coordinator, and went grocery shopping—a significant personal challenge. We compiled a master list of all she wanted or needed to do, which steadied and reassured her. Day by day, she was settling into her new world. As she expressed it: "I am building my life from the ground up."

The opportunity arose to accompany a friend on a week-long meditation and yoga retreat in the Bahamas. They planned to leave on Boxing Day, and we had no more than a week to prepare. Fran's energy was starting to flag again.

Fran was really tired today, but she allowed me to get her going with packing. She trusts me to pick what she needs to do next and urge her to accomplish it. She has done a lot today, and will be even more tired when we meet later. I don't want to push her any further. She deserves some quiet time.

I felt guilty for pushing her so much, but it was necessary and she valued my help.

Fran:	What will we do this afternoon? Pack? Or nap?
Martin:	No naps! You slept well last night. What time are you going out today? I need you back by 2 p.m. We have lots of packing to do. And you will be tired by 6 p.m. so the more we do this afternoon the better. I know I yap at your heels, but only because you are leaving soon and there's still a lot to do. Maybe I should ease off nagging you.
Fran:	Just be you. Somebody has to get me ready!

Swimming in Happy Water

One of the large Victorian houses nearby opened its doors to visitors at Christmas in aid of local charities.

Fran:	Do you wanna go to Swan Hall with me?
Martin:	Is that the Christmas tree house?
Fran:	Yes.. It's $5 but I don't think they'll charge for you..
Martin:	I'd love to! Christmas starts here!

We were on a video call as Fran arrived. I imagined she would end our call and take photographs to show me later, but she kept me on the line and even introduced me to the people on the door. "This is Marty, my friend from England. Do we need two tickets?" As Fran recalled later:

I took Marty with me through all the rooms. There were something like sixteen beautifully dressed Christmas trees. Marty took screenshots of what I was showing him and shared them on our social media. The pictures came out like beautiful watercolors, and ended up going all over the world!

On Christmas Eve I helped with the last of her preparations for the trip, which included paying bills and printing copies of her wellness plan and contact list. In the evening we shared a beer and exchanged gifts. Fran spent Christmas Day with friends, but we met for a video call late in the evening. It was the last we would share for over a week.

> We were both tired last night and weren't on for long. Fran had to be up at 3:30 a.m. today and we arranged that I'd call at 3:40 (my 8:40 a.m.) to make sure she was up. She was having a coffee and I made one here to keep her company until it was time for them to leave. She's had a rough time these past weeks: depression over her weight (it was down today but has been rising for a while now), Christmas, and anxieties over preparing for the Bahamas. I no longer worry over her trips. I'm not sure how easy it will be for us to keep in touch, but we are not panicking about it. We have grown so much. Last night Fran said how important I am to her: something about how a depressed goldfish swimming in happy water can't help but be affected. I said HAPPY WATER would be a great title for our next book!

Summary

Moving home is a stressful experience at any time. For Fran, it came at the end of a summer that had left her physically and emotionally exhausted, in severe pain, depressed, suicidal, and teetering on the edge of mania. It was a time of significant challenge for her, and for our relationship as friends. We made it through by holding to our shared values of trust, honesty, and open communication.

By reading our book you have become part of our personal journey, but as we said at the beginning this is not really about us at all. It is not about bipolar disorder, or even illness. It is about learning to accept one another for who we are. It is about embracing the journey we take together as friends, one step at a time. Be who you are. Do what you can. Embrace the journey.

Epilogue: Tumbling Around Humanly

Fran: you know.. it's pretty wonderful having someone so into you.. so caring.. so concerned.. so kind and compassionate.. someone who wants to know everything about you.. even and especially the yucky parts..

Martin: All of it is you. And you get to see my yucky bits too. I always feel safe. That's really what we give each other. Sure, we touch the edges, we mess up, we ache, we hurt sometimes. But we are here for each other.

Fran: tumbling around humanly..

It's true when I say I would be dead if Marty hadn't come along. So much hurt, so much pain, so much rejection, it made no sense to stay. Not only did he lend me his ear, he lent me his brain and lent me his heart. Mine were broken. He did not reach down a hand to pull me up from my dark hole. He came down and sat with me while I began rethreading, bit by bit, what could be mended. He let me baby step on his feet until I could dance on my own. To him it wasn't about getting me to climb out. It was about being with me in all of it. He fanned the tiny flame he saw inside me. The tiny bit that felt safe enough to grow again. Trust grew, kindness grew, love grew. I turned my face to the sky, felt the warmth of the sun, and opened.

Friends like Marty who are willing to be with me in the darkness are the ones who give me light. Yes there are medications. Yes there is therapy. Yes there is personal responsibility. But caring friendship is the best medicine of all. Then life begins to have purpose.

How do I help my friend? What should I try? What works? So many choices. So many possibilities. To me this book is less of a memoir than a menu. You would never order and eat everything on the menu if you went for a meal. You would choose.

Something familiar, perhaps. Or something new. Use our book like that. Choose something. A bit of this. A bit of that. And let that something ease another's pain.

There are many like me who live in invisible institutions of stigma, shame, and silence, the walls built by others from without, or by ourselves from within. Dismantling these walls invites connection. Be the gum on someone's shoe who has one foot inside and one foot outside. Stick around. It may not be easy but you can help someone make a life worth living. Maybe even save a life. One little bit by one little bit. A smile, a wink, a hello, a listening ear, a helping hand, a friendship all work together to interrupt the grasp of illness.

Be open and honest, with your friend and others you meet. Judge not, for misunderstandings abound. Acceptance, understanding, and kindness can pave another way. Let's.

Fran Houston
En route from Portland, Maine, to New York City
March 2016

Appendix

Personal Care Manual

Fran's personal care manual is a living document which she periodically reviews in collaboration with her care coordinator. Initially focusing on mania, the manual was later expanded to include depression.

Building the Personal Care Manual

Fran began by investigating how bipolar disorder affects her and those who know her. She sent the following e-mail to a number of trusted friends.

Dear friend

I am working on an early stages personal care manual to help me if I get into trouble again. Could you write down things you remember that I did, or what I was like, in the early stages of my mania? Maybe start with when I was full-blown manic and backtrack from there. I would like to compile a listing that is specific to me. It is important for me to do this so I catch mania before it happens again. I know you will be there for me if it does, as you have been, and that feels so very good.

Thanks, Fran

Fran compiled her own list of things that helped stabilise her mood; nourished her in body, soul, and mind; and protected her from becoming unwell. She also researched the symptoms and diagnostic criteria for her conditions. Once she had all the information she needed, she began to draft her care manual. "Putting it together didn't happen all at once," she recalls. "I would be going about my life and I would think 'Oh, this needs to go in.' People like me with mental illness tend to stop their personal care. Examples are laundry, showering, doing the dishes, and even eating. It either just gets too hard or we forget or it feels like it doesn't matter. Most of the things in the manual are simple but they are important." She drew up a Life Goal Statement, which summarises what she is aiming to achieve.

Fran reviews and updates her care manual on an ongoing basis as she discovers more about herself and what helps keep her healthy.

My Personal Care Manual

My Life Goal
To create a warm loving home—in my body, in my mind, in my dwelling, in my travels—by living and eating healthfully and choicefully.

What It Is About
My care manual lists things that are good for me, whether I am manic, depressed, pained, fatigued, or well. When I stop doing these things it means I am not well, and need support and encouragement to return to these basics. When I am sick I forget how important these things are and they are left undone. And then that hurts me even more.

Key Words
Highest good. Extreme self-care. Back to basics. No big projects. No new contracts. No grandiose ideas. Hunker down. Baby steps.

Give a Copy of This Care Manual to These People
[Named friends], [psychiatrist], [doctor], [care coordinator].

Stick to the Basics

- Take my medication.
- Monitor my mood.

- Attend my appointments (psychiatrist, doctor, care coordinator, acupuncture, osteopathy).
- Extreme self-care. Sleep well. Eat well. Exercise. Stay clean.

Daily Schedule

A regular schedule gives structure to my day and week.

- Sleep hygiene: aim to be in bed by 10 p.m. and wake at 7 a.m. and out of bed at 9 a.m. beginning the day with meditation.
- Meal schedule: 10 a.m. breakfast; 1 p.m. lunch; 3 p.m. snack; 5 p.m. dinner; 8 p.m. small snack.
- Bedtime routine.
- Morning routine.
- Aim to accomplish no more than 1 to 3 things from my list each day.

Self-Care

Slow down. Pay attention. Notice people and things. Don't talk about me all the time. No big projects. No new contracts. Practice not writing things down. Listen well. Accept. Let go. Spend time away from the computer. Take a walk.

Food and Drink

- Follow good meal habits. Pay attention to overeating and undereating.
- Use eating as a meditation rather than medication. Check in with myself.
- Alcohol in moderation.

Personal Hygiene

- Daily: shower, brush, floss, mouthwash.

High Tide, Low Tide

- Exercise daily: fitness class, walking, cycling and hiking (in summer).

Home Care

- Pretend a friend might come round at any moment. Be ready with self and home.
- Make my bed. Open the curtains. Get dressed.
- Change clothes regularly.
- Wash dishes.
- Clean, vacuum, dust, wipe, organize.
- Put away mail.
- Declutter. One thing per day out, three if possible.
- Water plants once a week.
- Launder regularly.
- Put away clothes.

Enrichment

Feeding Body, Mind, and Spirit

- Wear colorful clothes.
- Drink less coffee and more tea.
- Radio: classical music.
- TV: nature and other enriching programs.
- Visit art galleries, museums, theater, movies, music shows, and library.
- Make time for fun stuff.
- Add to my thankful list: one thing a day.

Social Engagement

- Call and get together with friends.
- Volunteer, engage in community.

Small Projects to Focus Creative Energies

- Learn a language: German, Spanish.
- Music: listening, singing, dancing.
- Art: drawing, coloring, photography.
- Writing: journal, poems, classes, memoir.

[Dated]
[Signed]

Travel Wellness Plan

Fran's wellness plan serves as a valuable reminder of healthy and unhealthy behaviours when she is away from home. We review the details for each trip, in collaboration with her care coordinator.

My Travel Wellness Plan

To: [Psychiatrist], [doctor], [care coordinator], [named friends].

This is my wellness plan for when I am away on vacation. I am giving you a copy because I feel safe with you, and I trust you to help me take care of myself. Please read it over now and ask me about anything you are not sure about. Keep it somewhere safe, in case you want to refer back to it later.

Thank you so much!

Things to Watch out For

Let me know if you feel I am exhibiting any of these behaviours. I might not want to hear what you are saying, so remind me of this document and that I asked you to help me take care of myself.

Signs of Mania

If I start behaving like this it might mean I am getting close to being manic, which isn't good for me.

- Talking really fast without regard for social norms.
- Not listening to others. Being argumentative, bossy, or intense.
- Talking obsessively about suicide.
- Spending a lot of money.
- Needing very little sleep and having lots of energy.

- Drinking too much (more than a couple of glasses of wine or beer a day).
- Lots of hand waving, lip quivering, and mouthing.
- Obsessive writing and rhyming.

Signs of Depression
If I start behaving like this it might indicate I am starting to get depressed.

- I keep saying that nothing is working.
- I don't want to do anything.
- I seem to be giving up.
- I am not showering, brushing my teeth, or caring for myself generally.

My Coping Skills
These are the things I need to do to look after myself. Please remind me if it seems I am not doing them.

- Taking my medication: [list of current medication, doses, and times of day].
- Meditating every day.
- Taking a walk at least every other day.
- Eating regularly and modestly.
- Paying attention to my personal hygiene.
- Drinking tea (instead of always coffee or alcohol).
- Taking time to enjoy art, music, and nature.

Actions for Me to Take
I may need reminding that I agreed to do the following things if people start to get concerned about me.

- Contact Marty and [friends] and tell them people are getting concerned about me.
- Contact my care coordinator.

- Contact my psychiatrist.
- Contact my doctor.
- Take Risperdal (to help stabilise my mood), but only after checking with my psychiatrist or doctor.
- Return home. Arrange for someone to pick me up.

Contact Details

These are people I trust, who know me and care about me. If you are concerned, please give them a call and let them know.

Martin Baker (Marty)
[Cell and landline telephone numbers, e-mail address.]

Close Friends
[Names, cell landline telephone numbers, e-mail addresses.]

My Care Coordinator
[Name, cell and landline telephone numbers, e-mail address.]

My Psychiatrist
[Name, cell and landline telephone numbers, e-mail address.]

My Doctor
[Name, cell and landline telephone numbers, e-mail address.]

Mental Health Crisis Hotlines
[Telephone numbers, web addresses.]

Permission

I give permission for the people in this document to talk to one another about me. Otherwise I may not get the care I need.

[Dated]
[Signed]

Resources and Further Reading

Support and Crisis Lines

Befrienders Worldwide
www.befrienders.org
A directory of international helplines.

IMAlive Online Crisis Network (US)
www.hopeline.com/online
1-800-442-HOPE (4673)

National Suicide Prevention Lifeline (US)
www.suicidepreventionlifeline.org
1-800-273-TALK (8255)

Samaritans (UK and Ireland)
www.samaritans.org
08457 90 90 90 (UK)
1850 60 90 90 (Republic of Ireland)

Sane (UK)
www.sane.org.uk
0300 304 7000

Organisations

ASHA International
www.myasha.org
ASHA International promotes personal, organizational, and community wellness through mental health education, training, and support.

Bipolar UK
www.bipolaruk.org
Bipolar UK is a national charity dedicated to supporting individuals with bipolar disorder, their families, and carers.

The Blurt Foundation
www.blurtitout.org
The Blurt Foundation helps those affected by depression.

Bring Change 2 Mind
www.bringchange2mind.org
Bring Change 2 Mind campaigns to end the stigma and discrimination surrounding mental illness.

Carers UK
www.carersuk.org
Carers UK offers advice, information, and support to carers.

Family Hope
www.familyhopeme.org
Based in Maine, Family Hope is a resource portal for people who support a loved one or friend living with mental illness.

The Maytree Respite Centre
www.maytree.org.uk
Based in London, Maytree aims to alleviate suffering and help people in suicidal crisis to re-engage with life and to restore hope.

Mind
www.mind.org.uk
Mind is a UK charity providing advice and support to empower people experiencing a mental health problem.

National Alliance on Mental Illness (NAMI)
www.nami.org
The largest grassroots mental health organization in the US.

NoStigmas
www.nostigmas.org
The NoStigmas Network offers online peer support, a directory of free and affordable resources, and informational and self-help articles and videos.

Rethink Mental Illness

www.rethink.org

Rethink Mental Illness offers help, hope, advice, and information to people with mental health problems and their carers.

SANE

www.sane.org.uk

SANE is a UK charity working to improve the quality of life for anyone affected by mental illness.

Stigma Fighters

www.stigmafighters.com

Stigma Fighters is a mental health non-profit organization dedicated to helping people living with mental illness.

Time to Change

www.time-to-change.org.uk

Time to Change is England's biggest programme to challenge mental health stigma and discrimination.

Books

Personal Accounts of Illness

Cardinal, Marie. *The Words to Say It: An Autobiographical Novel*. Cambridge, MA: VanVactor & Goodheart, 1983.

Close, Jessie, and Pete Earley. *Resilience: Two Sisters and a Story of Mental Illness*. New York: Grand Central Publishing, 2015.

Duke, Patty, and Gloria Hochman. *A Brilliant Madness: Living with Manic-depressive Illness*. New York: Bantam Books, 1992.

Fader, Sarah, ed. *Stigma Fighters Anthology*. Vol. 1. Booktrope, 2015.

Fader, Sarah, ed. *Stigma Fighters Anthology*. Vol. 2. Booktrope, 2016.

Jamison, Kay R. *An Unquiet Mind: A Memoir of Moods and Madness*. London: Picador, 1996.

Kelly, Rachel. *Black Rainbow: How Words Healed Me: My Journey through Depression*. Yellow Kite, 2014.

Klein, Michelle. *The Monster Inside: The Story of an Ordinary Girl in Extraordinary Circumstances*. Createspace, 2011.

Support and Caregiving

Fast, Julie A., and John D. Preston. *Loving Someone with Bipolar Disorder: Understanding and Helping Your Partner*. Oakland, CA: New Harbinger, 2004.

Last, Cynthia G. *When Someone You Love Is Bipolar: Help and Support for You and Your Partner*. New York: Guilford Press, 2009.

Otto, Michael W. *Living with Bipolar Disorder: A Guide for Individuals and Families*. New York: Oxford University Press, 2011.

Suicide Awareness

Jamison, Kay R. *Night Falls Fast: Understanding Suicide*. New York: Knopf, 1999.

Shneidman, Edwin S. *The Suicidal Mind*. New York: Oxford University Press, 1998.

Suicide: Are You Worried About Someone? PDF. Scottish Association for Mental Health. www.samh.org.uk/media/455024/suicide_are_worried_about _someone.pdf

Suicide: Living With Your Thoughts. PDF. Scottish Association for Mental Health. www.samh.org.uk/media/455004/samh_livingwithyourthough ts.pdf

Interpersonal Techniques

Evans, Gail. *Counselling Skills for Dummies: A Practical Guide to Becoming a Better Communicator and Listener*. Chichester: John Wiley, 2007.

Rosenberg, Marshall B. *Nonviolent Communication: A Language of Life*. Encinitas, CA: PuddleDancer Press, 2003.

Food and Health

Hanh, Nhat, and Lilian W. Y. Cheung. *Savor: Mindful Eating, Mindful Life*. New York: HarperOne, 2011.

Roth, Geneen. *Women Food and God: An Unexpected Path to Almost Everything*. London: Simon & Schuster, 2011.

Education and Training

Mental Health Awareness

Beating Bipolar
www.beatingbipolar.org
Beating Bipolar is an interactive Internet-based programme that aims to improve understanding of the condition.

Mental Health First Aid (MHFA)
www.mhfaengland.org (UK)
www.mentalhealthfirstaid.org (US)
www.mentalhealthfirstaid.ca (Canada)
Available in many countries, MHFA is an educational course which teaches people how to identify, understand, and help a person who may be developing a mental health problem.

Suicide Awareness and Intervention

Applied Suicide Intervention Skills Training (ASIST)
www.livingworks.net/programs/asist
Run by LivingWorks, ASIST is aimed at caregivers wanting to feel comfortable, confident, and competent in helping prevent the immediate risk of suicide. Other LivingWorks programs include esuicideTALK, SuicideTALK, SafeTALK, and SuicideCARE.

esuicideTALK
www.esuicidetalk.net
An online self-study exploration in suicide awareness, intended for all members of a community, ages fifteen and up.

High Tide, Low Tide

QPR Gatekeeper Training
www.qprinstitute.com
QPR Gatekeeper training (the acronym stands for Question, Persuade, Refer) is one of several suicide prevention training programs developed by the QPR Institute.

Internet Resources

Martin Baker and Fran Houston
The authors' official website is www.gumonmyshoe.com.

bpHope
www.bphope.com
bp Magazine is an award-winning quarterly mental health magazine focusing on bipolar disorder. The bpHope website offers information and guidance on symptoms, treatment options, and relationships; also a blog and online community forum.

Guided Meditation and Imagery
www.healthjourneys.com
www.chopracentermeditation.com
www.youtube.com (search for meditation, relaxation, and sleep)

Mindfulness-Based Stress Reduction (MBSR)
www.palousemindfulness.com

Wellness Recovery Action Plan (WRAP)
www.mentalhealthrecovery.com/wrap
Wellness Recovery Action Plan and WRAP are the registered trademarks for a recovery model authored and designed by Mary Ellen Copeland and The Copeland Center for Wellness and Recovery.

About the Authors

Martin Baker graduated in Pharmacy in 1983 and completed postgraduate research at King's College London. Despite this academic background, he had little experience of mental illness until a chance encounter online in 2011. His transatlantic relationship with American writer and photographer Fran Houston taught him about living with illness, but more importantly what it means to be a good friend. Despite living three thousand miles apart, he is now Fran's primary support and caregiver. Inspired to expand his knowledge and experience, Martin is engaged in the mental health community on both sides of the Atlantic. Certified in Mental Health First Aid and Applied Suicide Intervention Skills Training, he is a member of the National Alliance on Mental Illness, Mind, and Bipolar UK, and a registered Champion of Time to Change. Martin lives in the north-east of England with his wife and son.

Fran Houston graduated from the University of Tennessee, Knoxville, in 1991, and worked as a successful electrical engineer until she was overtaken by illness. She was diagnosed with major depression in 1994 and with bipolar disorder in 2003. She also has chronic fatigue syndrome (CFS/ME) and fibromyalgia. Inspired by Peaks Island's rich history, Fran interviewed and photographed long-time residents. Publication of *For the Love of Peaks: Island Portraits and Stories, a Collection* in 2010 led to her appearing on Maine Public Broadcasting Network and National Public Radio to discuss her book and the challenges of living with illness. She has been a columnist in the *Island Times*. Her Maine Voices Opinion Editorial appeared in the *Portland Press Herald / Maine Sunday Telegram* for Mental Health Awareness Week 2015. An open letter to her psychiatrist was published in *The Maine Review*. Fran lives with a beta fish named Jewells who often makes her laugh and gives her a reason for living. She loves her home town of Portland, Maine, and her many friends who love her dearly.

NORDLAND PUBLISHING
Follow the North Road.

nordlandpublishing.com
facebook.com/nordlandpublishing
nordlandpublishing.tumblr.com

NORDLAND
www.nordlandpublishing.com

CPSIA information can be obtained
at www.ICGtesting.com
Printed in the USA
FFHW01n1254070818
47696312-51328FF